REWIREMENT: REWIRING
THE WAY YOU THINK
ABOUT RETIREMENT!

D0830670

REWIREMENT: REWIRING THE WAY YOU THINK ABOUT RETIREMENT!

Jamie P. Hopkins

ISBN: 1983605298
ISBN-13: 9781983605291

I dedicate this book to my family: to my parents, who gave me opportunities to succeed in life; to my sisters, who encouraged me through the years; to my wife, Kathy, who is the light of my life; and to my wonderful children, who always put a smile on my face and represent the eternal hope that the future will be better than the past.

Contents

Why *Rewirement*? For years I have been working in my role as a professor and research director to positively impact America's retirement preparedness and retirement satisfaction. I came to the American College of Financial Services, the leader in financial services education, to help build an education program focused specifically on retirement income planning—the Retirement Income Certified Professional (RICP) designation. I recognized this as a great opportunity because I could see the need for specialized education by watching my family members and friends go through retirement. I could see that many of them really didn't know what to do. Although they had saved for this time for decades, they were making bad decisions, uninformed decisions, and sometimes even decisions based on fear. Even though the process of saving for retirement had been challenging at times, it was clear to me that making it through the duration of retirement was even more financially challenging.

But *why* was it so much more challenging than saving for retirement? What I realized was that retirees naturally rely on the kind of financial knowledge they know worked for them when saving for retirement. Once they enter the retirement phase and find that the need to spend is more important than the need to save, they find that many of those practical concepts just do not apply anymore. Investing for growth and investing for a secure retirement income are very different concepts.

To make sure I was not just looking at a number of anecdotal pieces of evidence from my friends and family, I engaged in a more comprehensive research project to gauge the retirement income planning literacy and knowledge of Americans. What I found was extremely troubling. Across the board, Americans performed poorly on the retirement income literacy quiz. But perhaps even more upsetting was that even those individuals with strong general financial planning knowledge about saving for retirement really did not demonstrate high levels of retirement income literacy. The study also found that poor literacy rates for retirement income planning can lead to a less-than-optimal retirement. People with low retirement income literacy rates were unhappier, felt more financially insecure, and did less quality planning. The power of literacy is real.

However, the study also showed that many people were really convinced that they did know the material. Why? Again, they were applying the same concepts they had learned about saving for retirement to the very different dynamic of spending in retirement. It just doesn't match up.

I then realized there is a huge hurdle holding Americans back from a more secure retirement, and it is the way they are thinking. The lack of understanding about the ways finances change in retirement combined with a sense of overconfidence based on years of successful saving leading up to retirement spell *trouble* with a capital *T*. It was at that time that the notion of "rewirement" was born. In order for people to retire successfully, they need to "rewire," or change the way they think about finances and retirement.

Acknowledgments

I want to acknowledge Professor David Littell for being a mentor to me in the retirement planning field. I also want to thank The American College of Financial Services for its dedication to education in the financial services profession. Lastly, I want to thank my colleague and good friend John Whitham for his editorial support and guidance for this book.

1

Introduction to Rewirement

Retirement planning is like hitting a moving target in the wind.

—JAMIE P. HOPKINS

Can you visualize your retirement? Most people cannot, yet they still retire cold turkey, with no plan in place. Just answering some simple questions can drastically improve your happiness and finances in retirement, but it likely requires to you "rewire" the way you think about retirement. *Rewirement* is the process of changing the way you think about retirement to overcome mental and behavioral hurdles holding you back from a more financially secure future.

Rewiring your mind to improve your retirement starts with a fairly simple exercise. Before you can do any planning, you need to visualize how you plan on spending your time in retirement. Do you know where you want to be, what you want to be doing, and whom you want at your side when you retire? Are you sinking into a faded blue beach chair on a white-sand beach while discussing your grandchildren's latest success stories with your spouse? Or perhaps you are with your friends on the back nine of your local golf course, gearing up for an eagle putt? Once you can visualize what you want in retirement, the next important question is *How will you attain these goals?* Retirement planning is like hitting a moving target in the wind. Your retirement goals will continue to evolve throughout your life, while retirement tools, laws, risks, and techniques will also continue to change over time. If you want to accomplish your goals, no matter how simple or complex, you need planning.

In addition to planning, you will need to overcome significant personal hurdles, misconceptions, and detrimental behavioral biases that derail you by taking proactive steps to rewire the way you think and act. You will need to set goals, save money, and understand the risks and roadblocks ahead of you.

The reality is that people are messy. Many of us are overconfident and underprepared to plan for our own retirement. In fact, most people are their own biggest roadblock to a financially secure and happy retirement. This is because a lot of the human aspects of decision-making and self-protection that work so wonderfully throughout our everyday lives actually backfire when it comes to retirement planning. These behavioral finance biases can cause you to make irrational financial decisions. So, to help ourselves, we often need to get out of our own way. And one way to get out of our own way is to set up a plan that takes us to where we need to go—a secure and happy retirement.

Retirement is a new phase in your life, something you have not lived through before. It takes a new mindset. But no matter how daunting the challenges are, you need to remember that you are in control—as long as you take the time to develop a comprehensive retirement plan. Research shows that those who proactively plan for retirement significantly improve their finances, retirement satisfaction, and overall happiness as compared to those who do not take active planning steps. People with financial plans accumulate nearly 250 percent more retirement savings than those without a financial plan in place. Good planning starts with good information. In order to meet your retirement goals, you need to have accurate information so that you can make informed decisions about your future. This often means overcoming misconceptions or hang-ups you may have about a variety of financial concepts.

One way to get out of your own way and improve your retirement is to automate your plan as much as possible to help avoid those behavioral finance biases that can get us off course. But what you automate, and how much, depends on where you are in your career. Millennials and those early in their careers need different investment tools and strategies than those in their mid-sixties. For younger individuals, automating savings is more important than for those nearing or already in retirement. For those in retirement, automating withdrawals and investment allocations can be more important.

It is also important to acknowledge that moving from the workforce into retirement can be financially, mentally, and emotionally challenging. It presents change and a new life phase never before experienced. This move requires you to rewire the way you think about life. You must prepare yourself for the unknowns ahead and be proactive to improve your quality of life. There is power and success in planning! Research has shown that those who plan for retirement end up with more money and are happier in retirement. If you want less money and less happiness, then plan on not planning. But for everyone else, a retirement plan is essential for this portion of your life. In fact, part of retirement planning is all about figuring out what to do when you can no longer make decisions and take care of yourself. If you plan on retiring and living to an extended age, you will need to be able to take care of yourself. If you do not engage in retirement planning, do not expect anyone else to do it all for you. In order to have a successful and enjoyable retirement on your own terms, you need to be proactive and take charge of your planning to set yourself up for the secure future that you want.

It is no secret that the United States is on the brink of a retirement crisis. The baby boomers are retiring in droves, nearly ten thousand a day, and will continue to do so for years to come. This workforce exodus is just the tip of the retirement crisis iceberg. The baby boomers, as a group, are wholly unprepared for retirement. They do not have the financial assets needed to retire and maintain their current quality of life. Perhaps even scarier is the fact that many soon-to-be retirees have no retirement income plan in place and have not sought out the help of a professional retirement planner. The lack of planning and savings will become even more evident in future years when these already financially unprepared retirees will face tremendous expenses for their health care and long-term care. By then it will be far too late to save additional money for retirement or to plan for these risks. Instead, retirees and people approaching retirement need to understand the strategies and tools available to make their limited accumulated savings and assets stretch out over a lifetime—and to manage the risks they face along the way. The good news is that this can be done by making smarter choices with regard to Social Security, Medicare, IRAs, and taxes by being proactive and executing a comprehensive plan. Planning will improve your retirement security and prepare you for the future so you can retire on your own terms.

Remember, retirement planning is complex and can take decades of saving and coordination, so it is never too early to start planning. The sooner you start, the more likely you are to be successful in meeting your retirement goals. People who create a retirement plan tend to be more successful, worry less about their finances, and report a higher satisfaction with their lives.

There is a lot you can do on your own, but don't be afraid to ask for help as well. Take the time to find a retirement advisor with solid credentials, like a Retirement Income Certified Professional (RICP) or a Certified Financial Planner (CFP). You wouldn't trust a doctor who hasn't had surgical training to perform surgery on you, so don't get a financial advisor who hasn't had retirement income training. Remember that you are in control of your retirement. As long as you make well-informed and carefully planned decisions, you can improve your retirement income security without saving even a dollar more!

This book will highlight the major risks, mental hurdles, and behavioral biases that can derail your retirement and provide a process to follow to create a well-developed plan. Whether you are just getting started in your first career or you can see the finish line, this book can help you live a more successful financial life and will help you become better prepared for what lies ahead. Specifically, for those of you at the beginning of your career, it will discuss essential saving, investing, and planning strategies to ensure that you can grow and obtain the investment portfolio nest egg that everyone wants. For those closer to retirement, just saving isn't enough. You need to turn your savings into a monthly paycheck. This book will provide the tools and techniques necessary for you to make more informed retirement planning decisions from this point forward, including how to turn your nest egg into sustainable retirement income.

This book will also explain some of the best investment tips, products, and retirement tools available today. Those preparing for retirement need to understand the tools available to them and how to use those tools in a systematic and efficient manner in relation to their retirement plan. For example, if you are planning for a long-term care event, the tools and techniques would likely be very different than if you are planning on purchasing a second home in retirement.

In the end, your retirement will be unique. By reading this book you will become better informed about where to begin your own retirement plan and better equipped to utilize tools and techniques tailored to your goals. Most importantly, the book will help you by rewiring the way you think about retirement. The reality is that most people want a financially secure future, and that is achievable, but it requires change and planning. While retirement and financial planning can be daunting, a proactive and intelligent approach can improve your life and the lives of your family members. Filled with expert tips, this book will clearly explain the various risks that can thwart a successful retirement plan. By better understanding the risks you face, you will be better able to visualize the steps you need to take to prepare yourself for retirement security.

2

Retirement Basics

WHAT IS RETIREMENT?

The trouble with retirement is that you never get a day off.

—ABE LEMONS, BASKETBALL COACH

I love the former University of Texas basketball coach Abe Lemons's quote about retirement planning. While whimsical, it also conjures feelings about how retirement takes over your life. But retirement does not mean the same thing to everyone. The reality is that even the term *retirement* is not easy to define. While most people view retirement as a time when they are no longer working and do not plan on returning to work, others continue to work in retirement.

Retirement is full of various challenges and opportunities. For many, retirement offers the freedom to engage in activities that were unattainable while working, but it also means leaving behind those consistent paychecks that everyone has grown accustomed to receiving for the past few decades. As such, life in retirement can be fundamentally different from other phases of your life. In a lot of ways, I see retirement as the time of your life when your employment is no longer the primary income source used to fund your day-to-day expenses. Instead, you are going to be your own boss, and you will need to supply the income and paychecks for yourself from savings, part-time work, Social Security, and other income sources.

Although you may no longer be employed in retirement, there is still work to be done. You need to have an actionable plan in place to turn your financial assets into a steady stream of income to meet your day-to-day expenses as well as your goals and long-term needs. Perhaps the most challenging part of retirement income planning is that you will need this income to last for an uncertain amount of time.

It is important to note that many people do want to continue working in retirement. Some people look at retirement as an opportunity to do volunteer work, while others want to continue employment in the form of a phased re- tirement, a bridge job, part-time employment, or even a whole new career (a so called "encore" career). If you are someone who plans to work in retirement, I say that is great! However, I also want to caution you. Many more people plan on working in retirement than actually end up working in retirement. This is important to understand, especially if part of your plan is to rely on contin- ued employment to fund your retirement. Other factors and risks to consider when relying on continued employment are that your company may downsize or you may become physically unable to work. With these considerations in mind, you will still want to be sure you have sufficient savings and income sources to handle a full departure from the workforce.

The answer to when and how to retire is not definitive for each individual either. Some people don't choose to retire at all but are forced into retirement due to caretaking responsibilities, company downsizing, health-related issues, or other life events. Other people retire when they feel they are financially ca- pable of meeting their lifestyle goals without continued employment. Then there are some for whom retirement may begin simply due to social norms or other anchor points. Anchor points can be socially or legally created. For example, if you see your family and friends all start to retire around age sixty- two, you may feel some pressure to join them in retirement. Following others into retirement without your own plan in place can be like following them off a bridge: maybe the water will be fine, but shouldn't you check first? The fact is that far too many people retire prematurely—meaning they are still able to work but do not yet have sufficient funds to meet their retirement income needs. Whether or not your decision to retire is voluntary, you should first have a retirement plan in place. Before you leave the workforce, you need to understand how you are going to fund your retirement and whether you can afford to do the things you want.

The reason defining retirement is such a challenge is because it is not one neatly organized thirty-year period that looks the same on day 1 as it does on day 10,957. Retirement is a continuum of life phases. Your life at sixty-five and your life at ninety-five will undoubtedly look very different. At sixty-five, you may still be very active—playing sports, running marathons, swimming, golfing, and traveling. While it is not impossible to run a marathon at age ninety-five (Fauja Singh of India has completed a number of marathons after age ninety and even after age one hundred), most people will likely experience declining health and activity levels over time.

Rewirement Alert

Don't think you have to adhere to traditional notions of retirement. Climb mountains, run marathons, volunteer at a charity, or start a business! Define retirement the way you want to live!

In some ways, retirement is better defined by dividing it into three distinct phases: the early, active "go-go" years; the aging-but-healthy "slow-go" years; and the end-of-life "no-go" years. Many people feel fine discussing and planning for the early phases of retirement. The "go-go" years are often the most expensive because every day is like a Saturday. And what day of the week do you spend the most money on today? For most people, the answer is Saturday. So the first few years of retirement can be more expensive for many. However, discussions about the late years of retirement regarding failing health, long-term care, nursing homes, Alzheimer's, and death are far more challenging as they force us to look at our fears about aging and our own mortality. For some people it is far more comfortable to avoid these discussions at all costs, even if it means placing their retirement plans and financial well-being at greater risk of failure. In retirement planning, ignorance is not bliss; it is a risk exaggerator. By failing to educate yourself on the risks you face in retirement, you increase the risk of future unhappiness and financial ruin. By learning about the common risks, setting up a plan, and executing it, you can maximize your happiness, your financial success, and your quality of life in retirement.

BEHAVIORAL BIASES: GETTING OUT OF YOUR OWN WAY

Investing is simple but not easy.

—WARREN BUFFETT, INVESTOR

Warren Buffett is widely regarded as one of the greatest investors and financial gurus of our time. His short-but-sweet quote about investing is very telling. In reality, a lot of retirement planning and investing techniques are not complex. However, that does not make them easy. Why is that? Well, for many people, the biggest hurdle to a financially secure and happy retirement is themselves. You can even go so far as to say that you are both your own biggest risk and your own biggest asset in retirement. So do yourself a huge favor and get out of the way!

But how do we do this? Mostly, it's planning ahead of time and recognizing our shortfalls. It's learning, and it's hiring others to help us when we can't help ourselves. Rewiring the way we think about investing and financial planning is crucial. You may have heard about efficient markets and that people are generally rational. But a lot of new research in a growing field of behavioral science and, more specifically, behavioral finance shows that people are people; we are messy and don't always make decisions in a manner that supports our best long-term interests. Remember that casinos are open all across the world, and they are very busy, so people must not be all that rational! So rewire the way you act, plan, and think to have a more successful retirement.

We often make irrational decisions like valuing short-term gains over long-term gains or going to extraordinary measures to avoid losses at the expense of gains. For many of us, we are also our own favorite expert - reading, learning, and absorbing information in a manner that only supports our current view of the world. Let's take a look at a few behavioral biases that can harm us as we plan for retirement.

First, there is the concept of anchoring, which we want to avoid. Anchoring is the irrational way we attach our thoughts and beliefs to a reference point.

For example, we know others retire at age sixty-two, so we then think that is a good time to retire. This is not based on any rational review of our own finances or even the other person's situation. We also may see a stock hit fifty dollars a share. So we think that stock is worth fifty dollars. Then, when we see it trading at twenty-five dollars, we think that is a good deal because it used to be fifty dollars. But it may not be a good deal; the twenty-five dollars probably reflects its current actual value. So what can we do about anchoring? We can challenge our perspectives, seek out other viewpoints, and search for that devil's advocate position. Ask yourself why you are doing something or why you hold a particular belief. Sometimes you may just realize it's because someone told you to or you think you read about it. So take the time to look it up, and do some research to see whether your belief holds true. With retirement, two of the biggest anchor points we need to avoid are that ages sixty-two and sixty-five are the "correct" retirement ages and that you should take Social Security as early as possible. Everyone's retirement age is different, and Social Security, more often than not, should be claimed past sixty-two.

Next, many people use mental accounting as a way to separate their money into separate accounts or uses. So you may think this savings account is for vacation and another is for credit card payments. Mental accounting is essentially a form of budgeting that allows people to assign assets to different needs. However, it is not all that logical or rational. Money is fungible. Meaning if you have two savings accounts, they are not really two separate piles of money that can be used for only two different expenses. Instead, you should try to use all your money in the most efficient manner. For instance, if you have a savings account earning one percent that you have mentally accounted as your vacation fund, but you also have ongoing credit card debt, you should use the savings account to pay off the credit card debt. That is the rational decision. So the main way to break away from this bad financial behavior is to realize that money, regardless of its account or intended use, is still just money. Money is money. So use money in the most efficient way possible, not just how you thought you wanted to use the money.

We also need to avoid overreacting to short-term changes. The stock market is too volatile to be fully rational. This is because far too many people overreact to changes in the market. If the market goes up or down, people often react to the changes. Instead, most of us should show patience and just ride out our plans. If we have sound investments and income plans in place, we shouldn't have to dramatically change our investments due to market changes. So this usually means we should put our investments on autopilot. Individual investors do worse than indexed funds and target date funds because individuals overreact. Instead of buying low and selling high, individuals panic and sell when the market drops and buy when the market goes up. So if you can't leave your investments alone, get out of your own way. Hire an investment professional to handle your investments, or pick investments like target date funds, managed accounts, or managed payout mutual funds that reallocate and manage your investments for you.

Another irrational behavior that can damage your retirement is called prospect theory. The idea is that losses have more emotional impact on us than gains do. So we are more upset about a 20 percent drop in our investments than we are happy about a 20 percent gain. This can lead to our avoiding short-term losses, payments, taxes, or other financial "pain" that might otherwise be good for us in the future. For instance, selling a stock at a loss can be a good thing, in some cases, if it offsets gains on other stocks; this is called tax-loss harvesting. Or it may be a good idea to pay extra taxes today in order to convert a traditional IRA to a Roth IRA in the future. But in both of those situations, we may still be hesitant to pay more or lock in a loss today, despite the fact that both could be good for our long-term financial stability. This can be hard to overcome. It requires a fundamental mindset change. You need to visualize the future value or benefit of the decision. As such, having a plan in place that shows the future value or benefit to your life can be helpful. The more we can visualize the future benefit, the more likely we will be able to suffer that short-term pain for a long-term gain.

Most Americans also suffer from low financial literacy rates and retirement planning illiteracy. As such, many people just do not have the knowledge to properly plan for retirement. In these situations, it can also be hard to recognize what we don't know and come to terms with it. In fact, a lot of research shows that overconfidence in one's ability leads to bad financial and investment decisions. Overconfidence is hard to overcome alone. The reality is that the more an individual trades his or her investments, the lower the returns become. You cannot beat the market. So just embrace it. Buy and hold. Don't get into daily management and investment trading. Overconfidence is a great reason why you should consider hiring a financial advisor.

Rewirement Alert

Anchoring, risk aversion, and overconfidence can lead many people down a path to financial ruin. Instead of relying on those strategies, rewire how you think about investing by automating as much as possible by hiring an advisor or using target date funds, indexed funds, or managed investment accounts.

This is by no means a comprehensive list of the behavioral biases that we may encounter. But many of the biases and negative behaviors we have can be overcome by a few different techniques. First, we must get a plan in place. If we have a plan for how we will save, invest, and live in retirement, we are more likely to stick to it. Second, we want to automate as much as possible. Behavioral scientists have shown that this is one of the best ways to overcome our negative biases. So automate your savings, debt payments, and investment strategy. Set up automatic payroll deductions for your 401(k), have your credit card bills paid automatically, buy a house and pay the mortgage, consider whole life insurance, and pick investments that don't need constant monitoring, like mutual funds and target date funds.

MAGIC RETIREMENT SAVINGS NUMBER

Money is numbers and numbers never end. If it takes money to be happy, your search for happiness will never end.

—BOB MARLEY, MUSICIAN AND ACTIVIST

One of the most popular questions I get asked is "How much do I need saved for retirement?" The reality is there is no answer to this question. What we need in retirement is income. However, for many people, their savings will be what supplies the income. So you may hear numbers like $1 million or $2 million. Realistically, that is much more money than most people need in investable assets for retirement. Nonetheless, for some, it's not nearly enough. Perhaps you have heard that people need a multiple of ten to twenty times their current income? While these rules of thumb can be helpful in bringing attention to retirement savings, the focus cannot be on accumulating a set amount of money on a specific date as that is not realistic or doable due to market volatility and fluctuations.

The focus of savings should really look at the individual retiree's unique goals, needs, risks, and income sources. In order to figure out how much you need for retirement, you need to first be able to visualize retirement and come up with realistic retirement expenses. Once you can estimate your expenses, you can then start figuring out how much income you need in retirement. Meeting your income needs and generating a steady paycheck is really the goal for retirement income planning, not just wealth accumulation. Furthermore, you need to consider all the assets at your disposal to meet your income needs, not just your investable assets. This means considering how you will use Social Security, your home equity, your pension, your 401(k), and your life insurance and whether you will keep working part time in retirement. Someone who works part time in retirement and has Social Security and a pension will often need far fewer investable assets to meet his or her retirement income needs than someone with the same income needs who has only Social Security and a 401(k). Remember that when saving for retirement, you should focus on all the income sources you have available to meet your retirement needs and not just your accumulated investable assets. So how much you should save is really tied to how much you want to spend in retirement.

Rewirement Alert

Remember that there is no magic retirement savings number. Far too many people focus on retiring when they hit a specific investment amount. Instead, remember that a secure retirement is all about reliable income, not a magic savings number.

When we are saving for retirement, our savings are supposed to replace our income to meet our needs at some future date. So how much we need to save depends on our retirement expenses, how many investment returns we expect to get in retirement, and how long we expect to be retired. So, for those who expect to work longer, invest more aggressively (in higher-yield investments like the stock market as compared to CDs and bonds), or have a shorter retirement, you can save less. For those who plan to start saving earlier, in your twenties as opposed to your thirties or forties, you can save a much lower percentage of your income each year and still meet your retirement goals. For those who plan to start saving in your early twenties, you may need to save only 6 percent a year if you invest aggressively to replace your income in retirement. However, for those who plan to wait until your thirties, that number may jump to around 10 to 12 percent a year. And for those who plan to wait until your forties, you may need to save more than 25 percent of your annual income for retirement. So, the lessons are to start saving as early as possible, automate your savings, and invest heavily in the stock market at an early age. And most importantly, while saving is crucial to a secure retirement, retirement planning is all about generating secure income streams to meet your needs.

RETIREMENT SAVINGS VEHICLES

A simple fact that is hard to learn is that the time to save money is when you have some.

—JOE MOORE, TV PERSONALITY

Retirement planning can start with your first job. As soon as you start making money, start putting some aside for the future. Really what you are doing is consumption smoothing. When you are earning money while working, you need to save money for when you can no longer work to earn money later in life. For most workers, the best way to save for retirement is with a 401(k), SEP IRA, SIMPLE IRA, defined benefit pension plan, traditional IRA, or Roth IRA. Many of these are sponsored by your employer, including 401(k) and defined benefit plans. The 401(k) plan has become the most popular employer-sponsored retirement planning savings vehicle. Typically, 401(k)s are set up to allow employees to defer their own salary into the account on a pretax basis, allowing them to receive a tax deduction for what they put into the account, and the employer also matches some of what the employee puts into the account. The employer's contribution is also tax deductible, meaning the employee does not pay income tax on it until money is withdrawn from the 401(k). Additionally, 401(k)s allow for investments to grow tax deferred, meaning you don't have to pay income taxes on these accounts and investments until the money is withdrawn later in retirement. For most people, the single thing you must do with a 401(k) is always take full advantage of any employer-matching contribution. This means you need to defer money into your 401(k) each year. However, the percentage you must defer to take full advantage of an employer-matching contribution differs from plan to plan, so talk to your HR department to figure out how much you need to defer. Most people should not stop here and will need to save more than just what the match requires, as it is often between 6 and 8 percent of your income—not enough to save for a financially secure retirement. Also, remember that the 401(k) is really just a tax-advantaged savings account; you also need to invest inside it. So pick investments that offer you a good opportunity to grow your wealth for retirement. Again, if you feel uncomfortable with doing this, hire an advisor, or pick a target date fund that matches the year you might retire.

Now, if you are self-employed, saving for retirement is a bit different. You will need to be more proactive in setting up a tax-advantaged savings vehicle that you can put money into for retirement. If you are self-employed, you should consider setting up—or at least consider talking to a professional about setting up—a SEP or SIMPLE. If you run a fairly large company, you could even consider a 401(k) or defined benefit plan, but they are much more expensive plans to run. So for most companies with fifty or fewer people, SEPs and SIMPLEs offer the best savings vehicle from a cost and time standpoint. One downside with both SEPs and SIMPLEs is that they have strict coverage rules, meaning that most employees will be covered by the plan. As such, they work best for small companies. Additionally, you often cannot save as much with a SEP or SIMPLE as you can with a 401(k). However, SEPs and SIMPLEs are cheap to maintain and run. They also have simple documents and almost no annual filing requirements.

In addition to SEPs and SIMPLEs, traditional IRAs and Roth IRAs are great retirement savings vehicles. Traditional IRAs are funded with tax-deductible contributions, and then you can pick almost any investment option you want. But IRAs have served more as a rollover vehicle rather than a savings vehicle. When you retire from work, you will likely transfer your employer savings in the 401(k) to an IRA. IRAs are great for savings and retirement, but they are subject to required minimum distributions at age 70.5 and can be funded only with a few thousand dollars each year. As such, they typically can't be your only savings vehicle.

Rewirement Alert

Just because you are using a 401(k) does not mean you cannot also use a Roth IRA or traditional IRA! Remember that depending on your income, you can save in a 401(k) at work and set up your own IRA outside to set aside additional money.

Most people are somewhat familiar with traditional IRAs, but fewer people are familiar or comfortable with Roth IRAs. I think Roth IRAs are a vastly underutilized retirement savings and investment vehicle. I actually blame tax professionals in part for the underutilized Roth IRA. Tax professionals often look to minimize taxes today, falling into classic behavioral finance biases. They may not realize that a Roth IRA can offer tax benefits, access to funds, ease of use, and retirement income benefits that are too attractive to ignore when compared to traditional IRAs and 401(k)s. Roth IRAs allow you to save for retirement and receive tax-free investment returns while retaining access to your funds for when you need them. A great bit of advice for younger savers is to use the 401(k) to get the match first and then save in Roth IRAs.

A Roth IRA is a tax-advantaged savings vehicle designed for retirement investments. A Roth IRA is funded with after-tax contributions, meaning you do not get any tax deduction for contributing to the account. Your contributions are then invested in an investment that you select, such as stocks, bonds, or mutual funds. Once these investments grow in value, you can receive the investment gains tax-free, which is an attractive benefit of the Roth. According to the 2018 tax rules, you can invest up to $5,500 a year in a Roth IRA; if you are over age fifty, you can put an additional $1,000 into a Roth IRA for a total of $6,500. This amount can be contributed for each spouse, even if only one spouse is working, assuming the spouses are filing joint returns. Setting up a Roth IRA can be accomplished rather quickly. It can be started online with companies like Vanguard or Fidelity or initiated with a financial advisor through most large financial institutions.

While you cannot contribute to a traditional IRA after age 70.5, there is no age limitation on contributing to a Roth IRA, meaning you can contribute after age 70.5. Additionally, Roth IRAs can be set up for minors who have some earned income of their own. If you have a child who is working during summers, you could help him or her set up a Roth IRA and sock away some investments. While you do need income to contribute to a Roth, there are some limits. If you earn too much money in a particular year, you may not be allowed to contribute to a Roth IRA for that specific year. In 2018, for single filers, your ability to contribute to a Roth phases out once you hit $120,000 and completely maxes out at the $135,000 level. For those married and filing jointly, the phase-out range for Roth IRA contributions is $189,000 to $199,000. The income limits in 2017 were slightly lower: $186,000 to $196,000 for those married and filing jointly and $118,000 to $133,000 for single filers. Also, you can contribute to a Roth IRA in addition to your 401(k) each year—it's not an either-or decision. Most working Americans earn under those limits and are eligible to contribute to a Roth IRA.

What are the benefits of a Roth IRA?

- **Tax-Free Growth**: The main benefit of a Roth IRA is that your investments grow tax-free. However, you do need to meet a few conditions to receive the investment growth income tax-free. First, you need to have had a Roth IRA in existence for at least five years. Second, for a tax-free and penalty-free distribution of investment gains, one of the following conditions needs to be met: reaching age 59.5, death, disability, or incurring $10,000 of qualified first-time home-buying expenses.

- **Access to Funds**: While tax-free growth is fantastic, there are additional benefits of a Roth IRA. One of these benefits is the easy access you have to your own contributions to the Roth IRA. For instance, if you put $5,000 dollars into a Roth IRA and invest it in stocks and the value grows to $10,000, you can still withdraw your initial investment of $5,000 at any time without paying income taxes or penalties. This is because Roth IRA withdrawals allow you to withdraw your contributions first before having to tap into any of the investment gains. This is a great feature that does not exist with a 401(k) or traditional IRA because withdrawals of contributions to deductible accounts typically generate income taxes owed and a penalty tax of 10 percent if the withdrawal takes place before age 59.5. This Roth IRA feature gives people more access to their own money, more liquidity, and more flexibility. In fact, a Roth IRA can serve as a type of emergency fund because you have immediate and tax-free access to your savings.

- **Lower Taxes in Retirement**: Roth IRAs also offer great tax savings in retirement. Because Roth IRA withdrawals of both contributions and investment gains are income tax–free when taken in retirement, they do not increase a retiree's tax liability, tax rate, Medicare premiums, or Social Security taxes. The tax-free nature of Roth IRAs can be very beneficial.

- **No RMDs**: Another benefit of a Roth IRA is that the account balance is not subjected to required minimum distributions after the owner of the account reaches age 70.5. Most other retirement accounts, like 401(k)s and traditional IRAs, are subject to required minimum distributions. With a Roth IRA, seniors have more control over when they spend their money and are not forced to take withdrawals. This also allows the money to remain invested and continue to grow in a tax-free vehicle for a longer period of time.

Roth IRAs offer a number of tax benefits, retirement savings opportunities, and liquidity benefits that often go underappreciated. Remember that you can still set up a Roth IRA for 2017 by contributing before the tax return due date in April. Don't think it is too late to start using this valuable savings vehicle. If it all feels a bit overwhelming, find a good financial advisor who can help you to set up a plan and invest for your future with a Roth IRA.

In essence, there are three ways to get money into a Roth IRA. First, you can make annual contributions to the Roth IRA. For 2017 and 2018, the total contributions you can make to traditional IRAs and Roth IRAs cannot be more than $5,500 if you are under age fifty and $6,500 if you are age fifty or older. Additionally, you cannot contribute more than your taxable compensation for a year. So, if you only earn $4,000 in 2017, you cannot put more than $4,000 into an account. However, there is an exception for the compensation limit if you file a joint tax return. If your spouse had enough taxable compensation, you can still contribute to a Roth IRA as long as the combined contributions for both spouses are not more than the taxable compensation listed on the joint tax return.

You can contribute to a Roth IRA for the previous year up until your tax return date. As such, you can still contribute to a Roth IRA for 2017 up until Tuesday, April 17, 2018 (the tax filing deadline for a 2017 return). You can also contribute to a Roth IRA for 2018 anytime in 2018 and up to the tax return date in 2019. However, again, Roth IRA contributions are phased out if you earn too much money.

In addition to contributing directly to a Roth IRA, money can be rolled over from a Roth account into a 401(k) or 403(b) plan. There is no limitation as to how much can be rolled over from a 401(k) or 403(b) Roth account to a Roth IRA in a given year. However, there are other limitations that could apply inside the plan that could limit your ability to roll over money while still working, as many plans do not allow for in-service distributions.

Lastly, you can get money into a Roth IRA by way of a conversion. Traditional IRAs and qualified plans can be converted into a Roth IRA. By converting a traditional IRA to a Roth IRA, any untaxed amounts that are rolled over or transferred to the Roth IRA are subject to income taxation. To convert money to an IRA and have the taxable income included in a given year, the conversion must take place by December 31. So if you want to convert an IRA to a Roth IRA for 2018 and have that income included for 2018, the conversion must take place by December 31, 2018. However, you may not know your full tax liability for months. As such, under the previous tax laws you could essentially undo this transaction with something called a recharacterization if the conversion subjected you to unfavorable tax consequences. With a recharacterization you could undo the transaction and not owe the income taxes on the conversion by having any converted money sent back to the original IRA or account. You could do the recharacterization of a Roth conversion up until your tax return date plus extensions for a year. This gives you the ability to figure out your tax liability with the Roth IRA conversion and fix the transaction if it caused unwanted tax issues.

The tax reform bill has removed the ability to recharacterize any Roth IRA conversions done in 2018 and onward. However, you can still recharacterize your 2017 Roth IRA conversions up until October 15, 2018. As such, the last year to recharacterize a conversion will be for 2017. Recharacterizations are not completely removed in the new bill as the tax planning technique is still available for rolling out excess contributions to a Roth IRA. This is typically used if you contribute to a Roth IRA early in the year but then earn too much over the phase-out limits, thereby disqualifying yourself from being able to contribute to a Roth IRA for the year. As a result, you can undo the contribution without being subject to an excess contribution penalty tax by recharacterizing the contribution to an IRA. This strategy still remains viable after the tax law changes.

Under the old tax laws, taxpayers could engage in partial recharacterizations and could pinpoint the exact amount to convert and recharacterize to use up the top of a tax bracket, often called a bracket bumping conversion. Partially recharacterizing a conversion helped taxpayers stay in one tax bracket and not jump into another one if the conversion pushed their income up too much. This was helpful because the conversion needed to be done before someone learned of his or her full tax liability for a given year. However, this strategy was removed by the recent tax law changes.

Rewirement Alert

Don't be afraid of paying taxes today! Convert money from a traditional IRA to a Roth IRA when you are in a year of lower taxes. Look for those years when you lost your job, switched jobs, went to part-time employment, or retired as they can cause you to earn less and be in a lower income tax bracket.

Roth IRA contributions and conversions remain valuable planning options. In fact, if your tax bracket is lower than normal due to the new tax laws, you should talk to an advisor or accountant about Roth conversions as they are more valuable when you are in a lower tax rate environment. As you may have noticed, I spend a lot of time talking about Roth IRAs. This is because I think they are vastly underutilized retirement savings vehicles. Biases against paying taxes today often hold people back from taking full advantage of Roth savings. Rewire the way you think about taxes. Sometimes it can be a good idea to pay taxes today to get tax-free growth like in a Roth IRA!

SAVING VERSUS INVESTING

How many millionaires do you know who have become wealthy by investing in savings accounts? I rest my case.

—ROBERT G. ALLEN, AUTHOR AND INVESTOR

Setting money aside in IRAs and 401(k)s is just one part of preparing for a financially secure future. But you need to invest this money in assets that will provide you solid returns over time. This often means taking a risk.

When you set money aside or cut back expenditures after budgeting, you are saving money. However, saving money is very different than investing money. First, we need to save money so we can invest it. So *Save! Save! Save!* which enables you to *Invest! Invest! Invest!* which allows you to *Spend! Spend! Spend!* in retirement.

Without saving, we do not have money to invest, and without investments, we won't have the money to spend in retirement. When investing for retirement, automate as much as possible by hiring a financial advisor. Research shows that the most valuable reason to hire someone is so that he or she can act as a less emotional third party. The financial advisor keeps you from engaging in those damaging behavioral biases when markets take a downturn. I know very few people want to hire someone else to keep them from making bad decisions, but in a lot of ways that is what you are doing. There is tremendous value in having a third party assist you in your planning.

Research also shows that the more transactions or investment trades an individual makes, the lower his or her total returns are compared to those who do not trade. So the more you mess with your own investments, the worse you make them. Consider using indexed funds, mutual funds, and managed accounts to automate your savings. While they may not be the absolutely most efficient investments, they will most likely far outperform what you will do on your own.

Remember that there is a difference between investing and saving. Furthermore, speculating is entirely different. You can do some speculating with your funds, but it should be limited. For instance, if you want to buy Bitcoin or another cryptocurrency, this is really speculation. It is not investing in the true sense. There is no way to model or project returns. Instead, you are just speculating that the value of the asset will increase over time. Speculating can provide huge rewards but comes with great risk. As such, you should keep speculating in your portfolio to a small amount, typically between 1 and 5 percent of your assets. Really, when speculating, you need to ask yourself whether you can stomach the asset becoming worthless and losing all the money in it. If you can't, then you shouldn't be buying it. We save money so that we can invest it—and eventually spend it in retirement!

PROPER INSURANCE COVERAGE

Fun is like life insurance; the older you get, the more it costs.

—FRANK MCKINNEY, JOURNALIST AND CARTOONIST

Saving and investing at an early age are beneficial, but all our good work can be undone if we do not have the proper risk management tools in place. I will cover different insurance products later on, but a brief discussion on having the right amount of insurance is worth the time now. While not all risk management tools are insurance products, many of the most popular and useful risk management tools are insurance products. There are two types of insurance you may not be forced to get that you should look into. Most people are forced to get car insurance, health insurance, and homeowner's insurance. You should make sure you have the right type and amount of insurance, but with life insurance and disability insurance, the onus to go out and get the policies is yours.

Life insurance is an extremely valuable risk management tool that can pull double or even triple duty with your planning. Life insurance, especially term insurance, is an extremely valuable tool to protect your family. If you have a spouse, kids, or other dependents, you should speak with a professional about life insurance. Life insurance, at its core, is really about taking care of others. It is about replacing your value, at least monetarily speaking, when you pass away to provide for someone else. If you get married, have kids, or run your own business, life insurance is a must. Nonworking spouses should not be ignored either. It is often a good idea to get insurance on both spouses. Once you get further down your planning path, you may also want to consider a more complex life insurance product like a variable or whole life product. Permanent life insurance products can also come with a feature called cash value. Cash value can be a helpful way to build up some savings that can be accessed income tax–free at different times throughout your life.

You may have some disability insurance while working. So the first thing you must always do is check to see what is available. Social Security also provides disability insurance to most Americans. However, many people should consider purchasing their own individual disability insurance while working. Premiums (costs) vary significantly based on the policy, person, and area of the country. As such, it is always worthwhile to shop around. There are both short-term and long-term disability policies available.

Probably the most important thing about insurance is talking to a professional to do an insurance review of your situation. This will include life insurance, disability, long-term care, and property and casualty insurance. One tip for everyone is once you get married and have kids, life insurance is a must! Start off by considering term insurance as it is the most affordable when you are young. Permanent insurance has a place and can help build up a tax-free cash flow source in the policy's cash value. So, consider permanent insurance if you think you have a permanent life insurance need or are interested in the special tax treatment of cash value. Insurance really is about protecting you and your family. It can feel expensive, but life gets a lot more expensive if you don't have insurance and need it.

HOUSING IN RETIREMENT

There is nothing like staying at home for real comfort.

—JANE AUSTEN, AUTHOR

Owning a home has traditionally been a sign of financial stability throughout the world. Homeowners also tend to develop a strong sentimental attachment to their homes. This makes sense as we spend a lot of time there. But this is one area where retirees need to rewire their thinking. The home is an asset and can be used to support your retirement. But it often requires the homeowner to take some affirmative action that may be uncomfortable at first, like downsizing or considering a reverse mortgage.

Housing and retirement is probably my favorite retirement planning topic. Why? Because owning a home has always been part of the American dream. Your home is also where you spend the majority of your time and resources. For many people, where to live in retirement is perhaps the biggest decision to make. And housing wealth is often the largest asset many Americans have by the time they retire. However, behavioral biases sneak in when it comes to housing-in-retirement decisions, often causing people to be irrational. The home represents a sentimental asset that people are often unable to part with willingly.

When buying a home, you have probably heard the widely used phrase "location, location, location." What realtors mean by this is that identical homes may have very different prices depending upon location. What this often means to home buyers is that they may have to pay more to live close to work or be in the best school district. The right location may also mean the most potential for capital appreciation—an important consideration when the home is a long-term investment. In retirement, however, many of these considerations move to the background. In fact, retirees need a new mantra when making housing decisions: "cash flow, cash flow, cash flow." Cash flow is king in retirement. Without it, you cannot meet your retirement income needs.

However, many people are unwilling to tap into their home equity to support their retirement. It feels like a risk to them. And if you have Social Security income, Medicare covering your medical bills, and a home, you can probably make it through retirement. But I don't want you to just make it through retirement; I want you to *thrive* in retirement. This means changing the way you view the home. The home is a savings vehicle that also provides housing services. It is, though, a bad investment that generally just keeps pace with inflation. That does not mean buying a home is a bad decision, but from an investment return perspective, it's not a good or competitive investment.

Before focusing on cash flow, it is important to begin with what people want, since that drives spending needs in retirement. The reality is that most people want to age in place. A 2017 research article published in the *Journal of Financial Planning*, "The Effect of Low Reverse Mortgage Literacy on Usage of Home Equity in Retirement Income Plans," showed that the vast majority of homeowners—roughly 83 percent—wanted to age in place in their current homes for as long as possible. People feel a deep emotional attachment to their homes. This emotional aspect of homeownership cannot be ignored in retirement, but it also cannot be the only consideration. In many cases, the current home is not financially or functionally appropriate for the homeowner to live in throughout retirement.

In addition to wanting to age in place, homeowners do not want to backtrack in retirement from owning to renting. Only 5 percent of the survey respondents in the aforementioned study indicated a desire to rent if they were to move out of their homes in retirement. Once individuals own a home, most want to keep owning a home. Homeownership evokes a real sense of achievement and is still viewed as part of the American dream. Even in today's increasingly partisan world, homeownership remains a shared value across party lines. In a 2017 Zillow Housing Aspiration Report, roughly two-thirds of both

Republicans and Democrats reported that owning a home is essential to living the American dream.

Since most homeowners want to age in place and not rent, let's take a look at why "cash flow, cash flow, cash flow" should replace "location, location, location" in choosing retirement housing. Cash flow can be improved in three ways: moving to free up cash flow, restricting debt obligations, or supplementing retirement income by tapping into home equity through a reverse mortgage.

The first housing strategy to improve cash flow is to move in order to free up equity or reduce costs. Downsizing is probably the most common housing decision made in order to free up cash as many retirees are living in homes that are too large, too expensive, and not fit for senior living. Downsizing to a more economical home that allows for aging in place can be a viable strategy because it helps to reduce ongoing costs and, at the same time, frees up home equity to support a more comfortable standard of living in retirement.

Closely related to downsizing is relocating. Relocating may mean moving to a more expensive house but in a less expensive area, perhaps even to a new state or country. When selling a house and relocating to a new area, it is important to look at the total cost associated with moving, including changes in taxes. Some states, like Pennsylvania, provide good tax incentives for seniors to relocate by not taxing pension and Social Security income, which can increase cash flow. However, the decision to relocate needs to be carefully examined because it is almost impossible to reverse. If you sell your home and move to a new state, it is unlikely you will be able to repurchase your old home and move back if you don't like the new area.

The second retiree housing cash flow factor is debt management. While freeing up cash flow and equity can be achieved through downsizing and relocating, taking strategic measures to deal with an existing mortgage can also improve a retiree's financial situation. Every year an increasing proportion of retirees are entering retirement with a mortgage; the required mortgage payments throughout retirement put a serious strain on cash flow. These mortgage payments can cause a substantial financial burden and risk for the retiree. To address this problem, some people try to make extra payments and prepay the mortgage several years before or early in retirement. Most research shows, however, that this is not the best way to handle a mortgage and can actually be worse for a retiree than just continuing to make normal mortgage payments throughout retirement. One option is to lower monthly payments by refinancing at a lower interest rate. Another option is to embrace the mortgage and spread out the payments over a longer period of time. While getting a longer mortgage for a retiree may seem counterintuitive, it can actually improve cash flow by lowering monthly payments and, in many cases, increase the longevity of the homeowner's retirement portfolio.

With the home being the largest asset for many Americans, it needs to be used strategically to support a retirement, but retirees also need a place to live. While there are a variety of ways to strategically maximize your home equity, there are six main ways to tap into your home equity in retirement, including through downsizing, a sale-and-leaseback, a traditional home equity loan, a special purpose loan, home sharing, and reverse mortgages. All of these strategies have different benefits and can be used to support different retirement objectives.

First, you can downsize in retirement. While it is a very emotional decision to leave your own home—especially if it is where you raised your family and lived most of your life—it can be a very good financial decision. Downsizing can help you move into a more economically affordable home. It could thus reduce a variety of home-related expenditures like heating, cooling, cleaning, and property taxes. Additionally, downsizing can free up home equity if you move into a cheaper home. You could then put that money to work for you by investing it or spending it to meet your retirement income needs.

Rewirement Alert

Overcome your sentimental attachment to your home. Don't think of it as an asset of last resort. Put your home equity to work for you early in retirement by downsizing or setting up a reverse mortgage.

If you decide you want to live in place, there are a variety of other ways to tap into your home equity without moving. You could engage in a sale-and-leaseback agreement. This type of agreement is often entered into with family members, whereby the children buy the home, providing the parents with an influx of cash, and still allow the parents to remain in the home. There can be benefits for the children also as they receive payments from the parents for rent and possible tax deductions.

If you do not want to move or sell your home, you could consider home sharing. This is a *Golden Girls*–type scenario. You can essentially rent out your home to other retirees, perhaps friends or family members. This can create an influx of cash for you, help cut down on certain expenses, and provide companionship. If you need help, there are home sharing companies that can help facilitate the agreements and find roommates in most states.

Another way to tap into your home equity without relocating is to engage in some type of home equity loan. There are a variety of ways you can take out a loan against your home. First, there is the traditional home equity loan. These can be useful for short-term expenditures in retirement. The downside of taking out a traditional home equity loan in retirement is that you have now just built in a new expense—the loan repayment—that must be met, or you could lose your home.

Another option could be a special purpose loan. These are not available to everyone and are very state law specific. However, some states offer special purpose home equity loans to be used for things like paying off property taxes or long-term care. You will need to look at your local laws to determine whether these are available.

Rewirement Alert

You probably have a negative view of reverse mortgages. I implore you to change your thinking about them. Reverse mortgages are not just for cash-poor, house-rich people but can benefit millions of retirees.

Lastly, and perhaps most importantly for retirement income planning, is the reverse mortgage option. Let me preface this by pleading with you to continue to read and not give in to your urge to skip the discussion of reverse mortgages because you have heard negative things about them. While there are risks with utilizing a reverse mortgage, if properly used, it can be one of the best features of your retirement income plan. A reverse mortgage is, in some ways, very simple. The lender gives you a payment in the form of a lump sum, tenure option, or line of credit. That amount is the debt that you owe the lender and will begin to grow at the applicable interest rate at the time, similar to a traditional mortgage. However, with a reverse mortgage, no payments are required while you are alive and still living in the home. Instead, the reverse mortgage continues to grow over time, essentially paying back the loan with your remaining home equity.

In the past, many people used reverse mortgages incorrectly by relying upon them as a last resort in retirement. In fact, you have probably heard people say to use a reverse mortgage only as a last resort. However, research has shown that using a reverse mortgage as a true last resort once all other assets are gone is the worst way to use your home equity. In many cases, this use of reverse mortgages just makes a bad situation worse—people run out of money, poorly spend the reverse mortgage payments, cannot meet their property and insurance taxes, and lose their homes. With a reverse mortgage, no mortgage, or a traditional forward mortgage, if you can't pay your bills or taxes, you can lose your home. Instead of being used as a default, last resort option, reverse mortgages should be used near the beginning of your retirement, either as a buffer against bad markets or as the first source of your retirement income. Research shows that these are the two most effective uses of reverse mortgages and can substantially improve your retirement security.

I see that reverse mortgages can be used in a number of ways in retirement. A reverse mortgage can be used to help cash flow for a retiree with limited income sources, can be used as a tax-efficient cash flow source because the reverse proceeds are not taxed at time of distribution, and can help someone fund Roth conversions. Additionally, a reverse mortgage can be used strategically in a coordinated withdrawal fashion with a retirement income portfolio. The idea is to utilize your home equity in down market years so that you do not exacerbate the spend-down rate of your retirement assets. There is also a program called the Home Equity Conversion Mortgage (HECM) for Purchase, which allows seniors to purchase a home with a reverse mortgage. This can be a good way for a senior to buy a home as the senior does not have to take out a traditional loan, which has monthly required mortgage payments, which the HECM for Purchase does not. And with an HECM for Purchase, the homeowner would put down about 50 percent cash and fund the other half with the HECM for Purchase loan.

I think there are three distinct situations when a homeowner should consider a reverse mortgage: First, anytime someone over age 62 is relocating and buying a new house. I think looking at the HECM for Purchase program in comparison to other options is prudent. This may not be the right solution, but it could be. Second, for anyone carrying a traditional mortgage into retirement, a reverse mortgage can be a good way to pay off a traditional mortgage and create flexibility in cash flow. The reverse mortgage essentially allows you to make monthly mortgage payments if you want, and in months that you don't want to make a payment, you don't have to. Lastly, anyone doing a systematic withdrawal strategy in retirement should at least consider home equity as an asset.

Now, there are more complex and coordinated strategies out there too. For example, a reverse mortgage option can help you to defer Social Security. If you need income at 62 when you retire but don't want to take Social Security early, you could take a payment option from a reverse mortgage to provide you with the same amount of income. The reverse mortgage would likely charge a rate of around 4.5 percent in today's market, while Social Security gives you guaranteed increases of 7 to 8 percent per year when you defer benefits. You can run the math. It's fairly simple. If I can borrow at 4.5 percent and get 8 percent increases elsewhere, it works out. Now, as interest rates rise, borrowing from your home equity to support Social Security deferral won't be an effective strategy.

While many people find it mentally and emotionally difficult to use a reverse mortgage as their primary income source early in retirement, more people feel comfortable using the line of credit option as a protection against bad market returns. The idea is somewhat simple. At age sixty-two, you can set up a line of credit. At this point, you have not withdrawn anything from your home equity, so the loan will not continue to grow. However, your line of credit will continue to grow. If the market suffers a bad year and your investments plummet, you can take an immediate withdrawal from the line of credit, avoiding a large withdrawal from your investments when they are at a low point. This can significantly improve your retirement income security. In fact, if the market rebounds in a year or two, you can always repay your reverse mortgage (the amount you borrowed from the line of credit plus interest) and still keep the line of credit open. Using your home equity strategically (i.e., through a reverse mortgage) early in retirement can help you to defer Social Security and avoid withdrawals from your investments in bad markets.

The best use of home equity and a reverse mortgage line of credit is in diversifying your home equity. While you may think your home was a great investment—and it might have been—most US homes only keep pace with inflation and offer no other real investment growth. Furthermore, your home is a very illiquid asset, as it can take months to sell, with a lot of your savings and wealth tied into it. This is an amazing phenomenon—that most people put their money in an illiquid and low-growth asset. However, if you use a reverse mortgage line of credit, you have now diversified your home equity into your house and a line of credit. The line of credit really creates liquidity in your home value at a very low cost. You don't have to use it if you don't need it. Borrowing always comes with a cost, and you will usually want to avoid debt if at all possible. But once you have your reverse mortgage line of credit set up, you can use your home equity to support your spending and income needs—especially if a 2008–2009-like market crash occurs again. Would you rather borrow from your line of credit at 4.5 percent for a year or sell when your stocks just crashed downward of 40 percent? The math, again, is simple. All you are doing is avoiding losses by using your assets to generate income in the most efficient manner possible.

Your home is a great source of pride and financial savings. Do not let your home just sit through your retirement without putting it to work for you. Whether you want to relocate or age in place, your home can be one of your most strategic retirement income assets, allowing you to reduce market risk, reduce longevity risk, and improve your overall retirement income security. Break that bias and think about the home as a strategic asset. Put your home equity to work for you, not the other way around!

3

Retirement Risks

DON'T RISK YOUR RETIREMENT

People need to understand the psychology of risk more than the mathematics of risk.

—PAUL GIBBONS, ECONOMIST

A secure retirement income plan starts with ensuring that your income needs and retirement goals can be achieved. During this process, you need to account for all the pitfalls and roadblocks that could derail an otherwise well-developed plan. While it may be incredibly daunting to evaluate every risk you could face in retirement, it must be done. By ignoring even one major risk, you could completely undermine your plan, leaving yourself without sufficient income to retire with financial independence and dignity. To aid your planning, you need to have at least a basic grasp of the risks you could face in retirement and be aware that you can beat back these risks with proper planning. However, the solutions offered will not necessarily fit into every plan, nor will they always be suitable for your specific situation. You need to personalize the risks and reevaluate how they impact your unique circumstances and plan. Really the most important part of reviewing risks is showing that active planning can help, which can help to get you over that mental block that you can't do anything to improve your situation.

In addition to personalizing, you will need to prioritize the risks. For example, if you have a history of health conditions, then your health care risk will be higher than that of some other retirees. As such, you would want to focus on making the correct Medicare coverage decisions and properly utilizing tax-preferred savings vehicles like health savings accounts (HSAs), which can help fund your out-of-pocket medical costs in retirement. If, on the other hand, you are more worried about how long people live in your family and about ultimately outliving your money, then you would be more interested in deferring Social Security benefits and purchasing longevity insurance. Ultimately, a good retirement income plan will prioritize and then address your risks. However, before you can do this, you need to understand the risks unique to your situation.

RISK OF UNDERSAVING FOR RETIREMENT

The question isn't at what age I want to retire, it's at what income.

—GEORGE FOREMAN, BOXER

As I mentioned before, the baby boomer generation is facing a massive retirement savings and income shortfall. A large part of the issue is due to a lack of savings and a lack of good overall retirement income planning. The good news is that even if you haven't saved enough to meet all your needs, you can still significantly improve your retirement security by setting out a retirement income plan and making good decisions now.

If you are still a while away from retirement, you can save a lot of money and improve your situation. The earlier you start saving, the better off you will be for retirement, as this gives your investments and money time to grow. Consider saving 10 percent of your salary for retirement. Also, make sure you roll over your employer-sponsored retirement accounts when you switch jobs, even if the amounts do not seem like much.

Unfortunately, as you start to near retirement, increased savings will have little impact on your retirement. You will need to focus on other areas of your planning, such as making good Social Security decisions, selecting the correct employer-sponsored-plan distribution option, avoiding early retirement, maximizing home equity, and taking advantage of some of the numerous tax benefits available for retirement planning.

While additional savings can never hurt, continuing to work can have a much bigger impact for those nearing retirement. Consider using your vacation days and spending some money in the last few years before retirement to avoid burnout. If you can avoid retiring early, or if you can continue to work for a year or two more than planned, this will improve your retirement security far more than simply saving a few thousand dollars one year before retirement.

For those who still have time to save, make sure you take advantage of contributions to your 401(k). If your 401(k) allows for salary deferrals, consider putting money aside for retirement. These contributions will be tax deductible, meaning you can defer taxes and the taxes on any investment growth inside your 401(k) until you take a distribution from the account. However, there are more things to consider. If your employer offers a matching contribution, make sure you are deferring enough of your salary to get the full employer match. Not taking advantage of the match is akin to leaving free money on the table. Also, pay attention to the investment options you choose inside the 401(k), and do not be too conservative. Many people fear market risk, but you need to be invested in equities to generate good returns in your 401(k).

In addition to employer-sponsored retirement plans, you can always create your own retirement plan with either a traditional or Roth IRA. You can put money into a traditional IRA in three different ways. First, you can roll over another account like your 401(k) balance into an IRA. Second, you can make a deductible IRA contribution. A deductible IRA contribution is limited to $5,500 in 2017 (an indexed number that can change from year to year—you will see a number of these indexed numbers in the book, and I will note them, but you will need to check the current year numbers before making any planning decisions), plus an additional $1,000 for those aged fifty and over. However, your ability to make a deductible IRA contribution is determined by your status as an active participant in an employer-sponsored retirement plan, your adjusted gross income, and your filing status. As such, if you participate in a 401(k) and earn too much money, you cannot make a deductible IRA contribution. The third way to put money away in a traditional IRA is to make a nondeductible IRA contribution that is subject to the same contribution limits; anyone who has earned income can make a contribution. While a nondeductible contribution will not help you reduce this year's taxes, there is still a benefit to making the contribution because any growth on the investments will be tax deferred. You can make a nondeductible contribution every year you work up to age 70.5, at which point you can no longer contribute to a traditional IRA.

Rewirement Alert

Too many self-employed people think it's too complicated or costly to set up their own retirement plan. In fact, the government created the SEP IRA and SIMPLE IRA for small business owners. These can be set up with little out-of-pocket cost and have minimal ongoing plan reporting and maintenance requirements. Consider using a SEP to shelter more of your income than you could each year in a traditional IRA or Roth IRA.

Another option to help you build your own retirement income savings plan is to use a Roth IRA. A Roth IRA offers different tax advantages than a traditional IRA. A traditional IRA is all about deferring taxes into the future. As such, the government requires you to start taking distributions after age 70.5 so that it can get some taxes from you. However, a Roth IRA is all about paying taxes upfront and allowing tax-free distributions later on in life. As such, there are no required minimum distributions from the account after age 70.5 because you will not owe the government any additional taxes. A Roth IRA can be a powerful planning vehicle. Similar to a traditional IRA, there are three main ways in which you can get money into a Roth IRA. First, you can roll over money from a qualified plan or another Roth IRA into a Roth IRA. A rollover can be a good way to move Roth savings or after-tax employee contributions in a 401(k) out into a Roth IRA.

Second, you can make annual contributions of $5,500 and the additional $1,000 after age fifty. However, there is no cap at age 70.5, so, if you still have qualifying income, you can continue to make Roth IRA contributions. All Roth IRA contributions are after tax and nondeductible. You pay taxes on your income and put it into a Roth IRA. The tax benefit is that all income you generate from your investments comes out tax-free, if you meet certain trigger and holding period requirements.

Remember that before age 59.5, there is a 10 percent penalty tax, often referred to as the 72(t) penalty tax, on distributions from your tax-advantaged retirement accounts, such as your 401(k) and IRAs. While there are a variety of exceptions to this 10 percent tax, be sure to consult a tax expert before taking any withdrawals from your tax-advantaged retirement plans, because the exceptions to the 10 percent tax are different among IRAs, 401(k)s, and other accounts. For instance, you can avoid the 10 percent tax on a distribution from an IRA for college education costs or $10,000 for first-time home-buying expenses. However, these exceptions do not apply to 401(k) distributions.

So, in order to withdraw Roth IRA investment gains tax-free, you need to keep investments in a Roth IRA for five years from the start of your first Roth IRA account, and you must hit age 59.5, die, become disabled, or be using a Roth IRA withdrawal for first-time home-buying expenses. However, you will still be able to access your retirement contributions without the 10 percent 72(t) penalty tax or ordinary income taxes. So, your money is your money in a Roth, but investment growth may be taxed if you don't wait long enough.

Rewirement Alert

Your money is fungible. Roth IRAs and 401(k) loans can serve as good ways for you to access money to pay for emergency expenses without being subject to penalty taxes. Think about your financial situation as a whole, and don't get sucked into mental accounting when you can use funds to reduce high-interest debt or other detrimental financial burdens.

Third, you can convert money from a qualified retirement plan or IRA into a Roth IRA. Conversions can be incredibly powerful retirement planning tools. In fact, you can improve your retirement security and have more money for retirement—without saving a single dollar more—just by doing conversions at the right time.

While I briefly mentioned Roth conversions earlier on, let's now take a look at how a Roth conversion works. First, you need to have money in an account that you can convert. Savings in an IRA can always be converted to a Roth and so can distributions from a qualified retirement plan. When you engage in a Roth conversion, you take into income the amount of money you want to convert from your IRA or qualified plan. You then pay income taxes on that amount as if it were ordinary income. However, you are not subject to the 10 percent early withdrawal penalty tax even if you do this before age 59.5. The money then goes into a Roth IRA and can grow income tax–free. There are no age or income limits to a Roth conversion, which means that anyone can do it!

While Roth conversions are not only about taxes, the tax-savings elements are often the driving factor. Because you have to pay taxes on what you were hoping were tax-deferred savings in an IRA or employer-sponsored plan, there is a painful aspect of a conversion. Many people do not like the idea of paying increased taxes today. In fact, some accountants will steer you away from Roth IRAs and conversions altogether, not fully grasping the value of a conversion. For most people, a Roth IRA conversion is a good tax technique if you can pay taxes at a low rate today. For instance, if you are let go from work halfway through the year, it may be a good year to consider a Roth conversion because your income and marginal tax rate will likely be lower. This helps you lock in lower taxes when possible. In some cases, you will just want to do a partial conversion and take advantage of whatever range is left in your low marginal tax bracket.

Another benefit of a Roth conversion or Roth savings is tax diversification. Many people have some tax-deferred savings and some taxable savings. However, far fewer have any Roth savings. By adding some Roth savings via a conversion, you can limit the risk of rising or falling tax rates in the future and better protect your savings.

A Roth IRA is also not subject to the required minimum distributions that start for tax-deferred accounts when you hit age 70.5. This enables the Roth IRA to continue to grow well past that point without being minimized by required minimum distributions. Additionally, any qualified distribution from the Roth IRA will not impact your income taxes. This can be very helpful later in life if you are trying to keep the taxation of your Social Security benefits at a minimum.

A Roth conversion can be very helpful in getting more money into tax-advantaged savings. The reason for this is that you can pay the taxes on the converted money from an outside account—and often should, if possible. This allows you to roll over the full amount from the converted account into the Roth IRA. This essentially works as a massive Roth IRA contribution. If you had a $100,000 IRA and converted it to a Roth IRA at a 25 percent tax bracket, you would expect to have a $75,000 Roth IRA. However, you can roll over the full $100,000 to the Roth IRA and pay the taxes from your bank account. That essentially allows you to make a $25,000 Roth IRA contribution for that year by paying the rollover taxes from outside the rollover funds. This can help someone with a lot of money saved in the bank get that money into a tax-advantaged savings vehicle.

A Roth IRA conversion can also create peace of mind for a retiree. When you have $500,000 in a 401(k) or IRA, the government owns part of it and part of any future earnings. Furthermore, it is hard to tell how much the government really owns because you don't know what the future taxes on it will be. However, with a Roth IRA, you own the whole account, so if you see a balance of $500,000, you can rest assured that you own 100 percent of that account and do not have to share it with the government in the future. You have already paid your taxes on this account. The removal of uncertain future taxes can be a nice benefit to increase your peace of mind when planning for retirement.

A Roth conversion can be used as a backdoor way to contribute to a Roth IRA. You cannot contribute directly to a Roth IRA if you make too much money. However, you can always make a nondeductible contribution to a traditional IRA if you have enough income and are below age 70.5. Then you can convert that contribution over to a Roth IRA immediately. This is often referred to as the backdoor Roth. Beware that this strategy does not work as effectively if you have tax-deferred money in an IRA as all your IRAs will be counted together when you do the conversion, and you will likely owe additional income taxes on the conversion. While Roth IRAs can be used effectively to increase your savings to avoid required minimum distributions and improve your retirement security, these strategies can be difficult to utilize properly. You should consider speaking with a retirement specialist to best maximize the advantages of a Roth IRA.

Take full advantage of Roth IRA or Roth 401(k) savings opportunities. If I could, I would have all my investment assets in a Roth IRA. Roth IRAs offer amazing benefits to young individuals with tax-deferred and likely tax-free growth. Ask your employer whether the company has a Roth 401(k) option, and if it does, take full advantage of it.

Take advantage of Roth IRA conversions too. By converting money from a 401(k) or IRA into a Roth IRA early in retirement, you take back control of your money. You no longer have to be subject to required minimum distribution rules throughout your retirement. As such, you can spend your money when you decide you want to instead of when the government tells you. Talk to a CPA or tax professional before doing a conversion so that you can take maximum advantage of tax bracket bumping strategies and so that you don't wind up paying more taxes than you need to. I don't like paying taxes, and I certainly don't want to pay more than is required.

LONGEVITY RISK

The 2,000-year-old man's secrets of longevity: 1) Don't run for a bus—there'll always be another. 2) Never, ever touch fried food. 3) Stay out of a Ferrari or any other small Italian car. 4) Eat fruit—a nectarine—even a rotten plum is good.

—MEL BROOKS, COMEDIAN AND FILMMAKER

I have always been a fan of Mel Brooks's movies, and his guide to longevity isn't bad either. Eat well, and don't overspend on cars. Honestly, I think one of the biggest financial missteps people make is buying cars that they can't afford.

Did your parents and grandparents live for a long time? If so, you may be worried about outliving your money in retirement. This is often referred to as longevity risk, which is really the risk of living longer than you expected to and potentially outliving your assets. No one can predict with 100 percent certainty what his or her life span will be. This uncertainty creates serious planning issues as your retirement income plan must be built to provide income for an uncertain amount of time. The average life expectancy for someone at age sixty-five is eighty-four years for males and eighty-six years for females. But remember that an average life expectancy is really just the midpoint here. That means that about half the population will die before these ages, and half will live past the average life expectancy, so if you just plan to live to the average life expectancy, you have only a 50 percent chance of being right. This means there is a serious likelihood that you may live past the average age and need income for a longer period of time. In fact, many people underestimate their life expectancy. Nearly 25 percent of people alive at age sixty-five will live to age ninety, and 10 percent will live past age ninety-five. There is a serious risk that you may need your retirement income assets to last twenty-five or thirty years. Additionally, with advances in medical treatment, it is no longer surprising to see people live past age one hundred. If medical treatment continues to improve, this could soon become the norm.

The uncertainty of your life expectancy cannot be fully eliminated. A good plan will customize a realistic life expectancy for you, taking into consideration your health, your family's health history, your socioeconomic status, and life expectancy tables. It is often a good idea to add a few years to the projection to build in a buffer zone to help protect against longevity risk. However, too big of a buffer zone could substantially reduce your quality of life in retirement because you may have earmarked too many assets for a time when you will not be alive to enjoy it. The buffer zone could be longer if you are a conservative person and very risk averse. However, less risk-averse people may feel comfortable with their own projected life expectancies. This does not mean that you should just pick age one hundred to be on the safe side. Remember that if you overestimate your life expectancy and decrease the amount of money you can spend while alive, you will be leaving assets unspent when you pass away. Also keep in mind that an average life expectancy is just a midpoint; this means that half the retirees will live past that age. You have only one life and one life expectancy, so make sure you are prepared to live until a very mature age.

There are many effective strategies to reduce the risk of outliving your retirement assets. One good way to protect against longevity risk is to transfer the risk. This can be accomplished by utilizing different sources of guaranteed lifetime income. First, Social Security will provide you with a lifetime income stream. This means that making the correct claiming decisions and maximizing the lifetime value of your Social Security benefits are crucial. To help protect against longevity risk, it is often advised that you defer claiming Social Security benefits as long as you continue to be eligible for a benefit increase, which is until age seventy. By deferring benefits, you will receive a larger monthly benefit for life, and the longer you live, the more valuable this benefit will be for your retirement. So don't fall into the trap of taking Social Security as soon as possible. Instead, figure out your life expectancy. If you think it is likely you'll live for a long time, consider deferring your benefits.

Another option would be to select a life annuity form of distribution from your employer-sponsored retirement plan. This would provide you with a guaranteed source of lifetime income that would continue payments no matter how long you lived. Far too many people take the lump-sum distribution option from their employer-sponsored plans. In fact, the annuity options offered inside your 401(k) or defined benefit plans may be far superior to anything that you could purchase on the open market. Additionally, annuities are insurance products that are often specifically designed to make lifetime payments. As such, the longer you live, the more payments you get. Review your distribution options, and make sure you are making the correct decision.

To reduce the risk of running out of money in retirement, consider deferring Social Security benefits to age seventy, pick the annuity distribution option from your 401(k) plan instead of a lump sum, buy a deferred annuity, and add a few buffer years to your projected life expectancy when planning how long your retirement will last.

Rewirement Alert

Most people underestimate their own life expectancy. Don't plan on dying young, but prepare for it. Plan on living a long time, and build a plan that supports it. Also, remember that 50 percent of people live past the average life expectancy!

If your employer does not offer a life annuity distribution option, or if you decide you want the lump sum for control, you could purchase a life annuity on the open market to provide you with lifetime income. Additionally, you could consider longevity insurance, a deferred annuity that annuitizes and begins to pay monthly income payments at a future date, say at age eighty-five. A type of longevity insurance called a qualified longevity annuity contract (QLAC) can now be held inside your IRA, allowing you to purchase deferred income and not be subject to required minimum distributions up until age eighty-five. There are limitations on how much QLAC you can purchase inside your IRA as the value of the QLAC is excluded from required minimum distributions at age 70.5. This annuity can be coupled with your other income streams to make sure you maintain your purchasing power and income needs if you begin to outlive your other assets. The downside is that many of these lifetime income products end when you die. However, you can purchase lifetime income annuities that either continue for the life of your spouse (or another third party) or provide a return of your premiums upon your death. Such options are add-ons and will make the annuity more expensive and reduce the amount of monthly income you will receive. Purchasing longevity insurance (QLAC) inside your IRA can help to protect you against running out of money in retirement and reduce your required minimum distributions at age 70.5.

A reverse mortgage can also be utilized to reduce the longevity risk as it offers a tenure payment option. Essentially, this distribution will pay you monthly payments for as long as you live in the house. The concern is if you live for a long time and eventually need long-term care in a facility: since you would no longer be living in the house, the monthly payments would cease. Reverse mortgages can be an effective retirement income tool to help reduce the risk of outliving one's money. In addition to a tenure option, reverse mortgages can be used early in retirement to create income as a bridge to help defer Social Security benefits, to reduce sequence of returns risk, and to help with Roth conversions.

Reverse mortgages and annuities can be powerful tools. However, both suffer from lower than expected uptake, due in part to some behavioral biases that hinder people from adopting the products. People like to be in control of their money and assets. As such, people are often hesitant with any strategy that is perceived as giving up control. Additionally, the products can be complex. This complexity can lead to misinformation about the products. With the exception of reverse mortgages, I don't think there is a more misunderstood product in existence. Consumers and regulators alike do not understand the product. This lack of understanding also inhibits usage. Lastly, the home is about the last great vestibule of wealth for many in retirement. As such, people hold onto it, despite the fact that it may not be a good financial decision.

If you decide to engage in a systematic withdrawal strategy, which will be discussed in detail later on, you could lower your withdrawal amount to make your investment portfolio last longer. For example, if you plan on taking out 6 percent of your investments each year to live on in retirement, you could drop that number down to 5 percent in order to make the assets last longer. In fact, a reduction in spending and your withdrawals just for a few years early in retirement can have a big impact on the longevity of your retirement portfolio. Additionally, you would take a distribution as a percentage of the account each and every year. For example, you could withdraw 5 percent of your account balances each year. Under this distribution strategy, you would never run out of money. However, your withdrawals would not be consistent, and there is no guarantee you would have enough money to meet your expenses each year. Reducing your spending and reducing portfolio withdrawals in down markets can help you extend the life of your retirement portfolio and keep you from running out of money later in life. Ultimately, picking a sustainable distribution strategy is crucial.

Lastly, you could create a contingency fund and set aside money specifically for later in retirement. A Roth IRA can be a good place to keep your contingency fund as it will grow tax-free and not be subject to required minimum distributions. Additionally, if you don't end up needing the money, a Roth IRA serves as an efficient estate planning vehicle as your heirs can inherit the account and take distributions from it without having to worry about income taxes.

Making sure you don't run out of money in retirement is not easy. The uncertain timeframe creates challenges. However, you can address these challenges by making smart decisions with your money. Don't be afraid to defer Social Security, use annuities, and reduce your withdrawals to make your money last longer!

INFLATION RISK

Inflation is as violent as a mugger, as frightening as an armed robber and as deadly as a hit man.

—RONALD REAGAN, PRESIDENT

My grandfather always reminds me that a hamburger used to cost him only ten cents when he was young and not the few dollars it costs today. While this is a familiar story to many people, the hidden lesson is the impact of inflation over a lifetime. While inflation typically only slightly increases the cost of goods and services from year to year, it represents a serious risk and challenge for retirement income planning as its impact is magnified over an extended period. For example, if an item costs $1.00 today, after one year of 5 percent inflation, it would cost $1.05. However, after ten years of 5 percent inflation, that same item would cost nearly $1.63. The impact of inflation is often referred to as a decline in purchasing power, as $1.00 will not buy as much in ten years as it does today. If a retirement income plan does not take into account inflation and the potential decline of purchasing power, it could meet the needs of the client early on but fail to meet those needs ten to fifteen years down the road. However, there are strategies that can be leveraged to better insulate a retirement income plan against the negative impacts of inflation.

The average US inflation rate from 1913 until 2013 was a mere 3.22 percent. However, international rates over this time were much higher. Furthermore, inflation rates in the United States have varied a lot over this period, with the highest thirty-year average being 5.44 percent and the lowest thirty-year average being 0.78 percent. While the cumulative impact of an average annual inflation between 0.78 percent and 5.44 percent over thirty years is huge, the United States has managed to avoid prolonged periods of hyperinflation over the past one hundred years—an issue that has plagued other countries like Brazil, which experienced annual inflation of 30,377 percent in 1990. (And no, that is not a typo!) Hyperinflation can have a tremendous impact on retirees, rapidly evaporating their purchasing power and leaving them without sufficient retirement income to meet their required expenses. While it is difficult to protect against hyperinflation because it would cause widespread shock to the entire financial system, inflation must be accounted for when planning for retirement.

Rewirement Alert

Don't underestimate the power of inflation. Even average inflation of roughly 3.5 percent per year will double your expenses over the course of retirement. So make sure you use an appropriate inflation projection when determining your expenses throughout retirement.

Just as inflation varies from country to country, inflation will also vary from state to state and across goods and services. For example, the cost of medical care over the last ten years has risen at a significantly faster rate than average inflation while food and clothing costs have risen at a slower rate. This distinction is incredibly important because retirees often spend more of their income on health care and living expenses, two areas that have seen higher-than-average annual inflation. To account for this retiree demographic inflation difference, an experimental inflation price index, the CPI-E, was created to monitor the impact of inflation on goods and services for the elderly.

Certain retirement income sources are better protected against inflation than others. For example, Social Security has an annual cost-of-living adjustment based on the consumer price index (CPI). This allows Social Security benefits to remain relatively immune to inflation. However, there have been proposed amendments to the current system to allow for cost-of-living adjustments based on the CPI-E index instead of the CPI to better protect retirees from inflation on items that directly reflect their spending habits. Delaying Social Security as long as possible is also a good way to protect against inflation risk because as benefits increase up to age seventy, a larger percentage of an individual's retirement income plan will be inflation protected. Consider using up your non-inflation-adjusted retirement assets first and deferring Social Security as long as possible to ensure that more of your retirement income is inflation protected.

Many financial products also offer an option to purchase inflation protection. For example, annuities often either allow you to purchase a set inflation increase in benefits—such as 5 percent per year—or allow inflation protection based on an index, like the CPI. Long-term care insurance also offers inflation protection to ensure the benefits do not lose their purchasing power over a long retirement. However, purchasing too much inflation protection can create an added cost that can end up reducing the total returns on the insurance or investment product for the retiree.

One of the best ways to reduce the potential risk of a decline in purchasing power in retirement due to inflation is to delay retirement as long as possible by continuing to work. Salaries typically adjust quickly due to high levels of inflation, and many jobs offer annual increases in pay to adjust for changes in the cost of living. If you are in a defined benefit plan, working as long as possible can help to protect your benefits, since they are often tied to your average highest three years of salary. You could potentially see a significant increase in benefits if inflation rises and your salary adjusts accordingly. Profit sharing and 401(k) account benefits will not adjust as rapidly if inflation increases during the last few years of employment. Delaying retirement can help you to protect against inflation, as your salary will likely adjust annually for changes in the cost of living.

Additionally, bonds, CDs, and other "safe" investments that guarantee a certain level of return can be significantly impacted by inflation. For example, if a bond offers 3.5 percent annual returns nominally but inflation is 4 percent per year, the bond's real interest rate is actually negative because the returns are not keeping up with inflation, resulting in a decline in purchasing power. Moreover, in recent years, bond rates have been historically low, increasing the risk that inflation could erode the purchasing power of the investment over time. However, the government does offer Treasury Inflation-Protected

Securities (TIPS), which are CIP-adjusted bonds designed to keep pace with inflation. TIPS can be used to create an inflation-protected retirement income plan. Inflation remains one of the great retirement risks, so having a plan to deal with it is important.

Equities are often referred to as the investor's most reliable hedge against inflation. Historically, equities have performed well over long periods, such as a thirty-year period, when compared to inflation. However, the performance of equities as a hedge against inflation begins to suffer when inflation exceeds 5 percent. Even in times of high inflation, equities still tend to perform better as inflation protection than traditional bonds. While equities are not a perfect hedge against high short-term inflation, over the long term, a well-diversified stock portfolio that includes consideration of international stocks can provide inflation protection.

Rewirement Alert

Many retirees think it's a safe investment choice to pull their money out of stocks and put their savings into CDs and cash. This can be a very risky strategy, however, because cash loses money every day when there is inflation. Instead, keep a well-diversified investment portfolio and consider using TIPS (Treasury Inflation-Protected Securities) if you want a safe investment that will keep pace with inflation.

There are other options to limit inflation risk in retirement, such as investing in dividend-paying equities, investing in commodities, or purchasing inflation-linked savings bonds or I Bonds. These are government-issued debt securities that are particularly well-positioned to handle inflation because they earn interest through a mix of inflation and fixed rates. However, the government does limit the amount of I Bonds an individual can purchase.

Additionally, home prices and rental income often adjust well for inflation. Tapping into home equity during retirement or having rental income as part of one's retirement income plan can help to offset some inflation concerns.

Inflation risk and the decline of purchasing power is a serious risk for soon-to-be retirees as future inflation rates remain unknown. As such, when planning for retirement, consider the long-term effects and the uncertainty of inflation over the expected period. For example, if someone plans to be retired for twenty years, it would be helpful for him or her to see the highest and lowest cumulative impacts of inflation rates in the United States for a twenty-year period. While inflation risk is a major concern, it can be mitigated through proper planning and by including inflation-protected investments in a retirement income plan.

OVERSPENDING CAN RUIN YOUR PLAN

I spent a lot of money on booze, birds, and fast cars. The rest I just squandered.

—GEORGE BEST, IRISH FOOTBALLER

Don't overspend your income! We are talking about the human element again. Overspending can easily undo even the best-laid retirement plan. Overspending can occur for a number of reasons, though two main reasons cause people to overspend: First, a person can just lack self-control when it comes to spending. Second, a person can misunderstand how much he or she can actually spend in retirement. It is the second one that we can rewire.

Many people think that if their stocks average 8 percent returns, they can withdraw their average returns from their retirement portfolios and not run out of money. However, if you withdraw 8 percent per year, adjusted for inflation, you will run out of money. In fact, the safe withdrawal rate in the United States is only 4 percent for thirty years, even though the average returns are much higher. This rule says that with a 50 percent stock and a 50 percent bond investment portfolio, you can withdraw only 4 percent of the portfolio each year—adjusted for inflation—if you do not want to run out of money in thirty years. Pay attention to the latest research on sustainable withdrawal rates, understand how the 4 percent rule works, and understand how sequence of withdrawals works. Understanding those factors will better prepare you to develop a sustainable withdrawal rate. Even a well-designed retirement income plan can be ruined quickly if you pull out too much money, especially early in retirement.

The reason why you can't spend your average returns is due to a unique investment risk that has huge implications for retirement income planning: sequence of returns risk. Investment returns are unpredictable and variable from year to year. The order of returns actually has a huge impact on the sustainability of a retirement portfolio that must be spent down in order to provide income. Large drops in the value of your investments in the first few years of your retirement can significantly add to the possibility of running out of money. Withdrawing money from an account while it is down can lock in the losses, and you may never be able to recover.

Rewirement Alert

Most people think if their investments average 8 percent returns a year, they can spend an average of 8 percent of their principal each year. However, this is not the case due to the sequence of returns. Bad investment returns and losses early in retirement can substantially lower the amount you can spend.

You can reduce the risk of excess withdrawals due to a poor sequence of investment returns early in retirement by reducing the volatility of your investment portfolio. By diversifying your investments, you can minimize the risk of large losses in the first few years of retirement. This means picking a well-diversified set of stocks and bonds that are not correlated with one another so that if one goes up, the other goes down. This can help normalize your returns over time. Additionally, adding in foreign stocks can help to reduce your volatility and increase your allowable withdrawal rate. In many cases, you will not need more than 10 percent invested in international stocks, which can usually be accomplished through a mutual fund.

Another way to generate more sustainable income is to set aside cash, bonds, an annuity, or home equity that can be utilized during the first few years of retirement in the event that the stock market drops significantly. Diversify your investments between large-cap stocks, small-cap stocks, bonds, and international stocks to increase the amount you can safely withdraw from your investment each year. This allows you to avoid withdrawing money from your assets while their overall value is down and helps you to extend the life span of your investments. A reverse mortgage line of credit is well designed for this task as you can tap into your home equity early in retirement if the stock market drops. However, if the market doesn't drop, you don't have to access the home equity and can save it for later in retirement.

Spending too much money is one area that you have a lot of control over. While you may want some flexibility to take additional withdrawals for un-expected expenses, maintaining the plan is important in the long run. This means you must pay careful attention to your spending. You may not have a lot of control over the market, and you may have only a limited ability to increase your income, but you always have the opportunity to reduce how much you spend.

Another way to avoid excess withdrawal risk is to engage in a flooring approach to retirement income planning. A flooring approach attempts to secure guaranteed income sources not impacted by stock market ups and downs. By switching your assets away from systematic withdrawals to guar-anteed monthly payments, you will have limited your ability to access money each month, reducing not only the excess withdrawal risk but also your overall access to liquid funds. Remember that you have control over excess withdraw-al risk, so set a good plan, and stick to it.

Social Security builds in a natural floor for most retirees. However, annui-ties can be another source of flooring and guaranteed monthly income pay-ments. There are thousands of variations of annuity products on the market. There are deferred annuities that begin payments at a future date and annui-ties that begin payments immediately. Furthermore, there are variable annui-ties that do adjust to market conditions and annuities that are locked in at the time of purchase. Annuities can last for one life, for a set period of time, or for joint lives (for as long as either you or your spouse is alive). There are also hun-dreds of riders that can be attached to annuity products, allowing for inflation protections and guaranteed lifetime withdrawals. Make sure you know how the annuity works and fits into your overall plan. All annuities are not created equal. So shop around and compare prices. If you are trying to buy monthly income payments, make sure you are getting the best deal you can. This is a great way to maximize your income!

You will likely hear or have heard negative things about annuities. Some of this is due to misinformation, and some of it is due to the fact that annuities can be complicated products that are not suited for every retirement plan. Make sure any annuity fits your goals and overall plan. Annuities have a place in retirement income planning and can make your retirement much more secure as they can provide you with monthly income and take market risk off the table.

Annuities can be confusing because they come in many varieties. If your goal is a predictable income stream for life, here are your primary options:

- **Income Annuities**: The simplest annuity product promises a regular (usually monthly) payment in exchange for a premium. For lifetime protection, you buy a life annuity that pays as long as you are alive. Couples may consider a joint annuity that pays as long as one of them is alive. Those who are concerned about an early death can get a death benefit, but it will reduce income payments. The deferred income annuity allows for the purchase of a specified income amount that begins in the future. Since investment risk becomes more dangerous as retirement approaches, removing some risk by prepurchasing a specified income can make sense. The income annuity locks into the strategy of converting an asset into income—and it is not reversible. This has advantages (simplicity and elimination of market risk), but it also has disadvantages (loss of liquidity and the flexibility to change strategies later). Income annuities will be combined with other strategies. So locking in is not a problem if flexibility is available elsewhere in the plan.

- **Deferred Annuities**: Another option for building an income stream in the future is a deferred annuity. During the deferral stage, the annuity value is based on the account balance, which is tied to underlying investment experience. Deferred fixed annuities promise a return described in the contract, and variable contracts allow for a selection of investment alternatives. The owner of a deferred annuity can choose to annuitize, which means the annuity becomes an income annuity at that point. With today's low-interest-rate environment, older deferred annuity contracts may have more favorable contract terms for converting the account into monthly income than a new contract— meaning that if you have an older contract, hang onto it. An important innovation with deferred annuities is the development of the guaranteed withdrawal benefit rider. The rider provides a guaranteed lifetime payment without your having to lock in as you do when annuitizing. When the income rider is turned on, you get a promise of lifetime income, but the account remains intact. If there is an early death or a change of heart, the remaining account balance can still be accessed. If the account value becomes zero, the rider continues to pay the promised income amount for a single or joint life.

Consider purchasing an annuity to take market risk off the table and set yourself up with monthly guaranteed income payments. When choosing an annuity, be clear about the primary purpose of the annuity, consider all available product options, pay attention to price, and look at the ratings of the insurance carrier.

Rewirement Alert

Many people dislike the idea of purchasing an annuity because they feel like they are giving up control of their money to an insurance company. But in reality, when you have more guaranteed income in retirement, you have more freedom to spend because you do not need to self-insure against your longevity.

It can be challenging to decide when to purchase an annuity. Annuity income can be purchased prior to retirement, at retirement, or in retirement.

There are good arguments for buying at each point, so a prudent alternative may be to continue to purchase income over time, starting well before retirement. Maybe the best reason to buy early is that you have met your goals and have the resources to buy the income you need. Both income annuities and deferred annuities with withdrawal benefit riders allow you to know with certainty the cost of income. Buying income by purchasing an annuity prior to retirement allows the value of the annuity to grow during the deferral period. This helps to reduce the cost of buying that income for retirement. You can reduce risk and build an income stream prior to retirement at the time that volatility can have the largest negative impact on retirement security. Some products, specifically deferred annuities with a guaranteed withdrawal benefit rider, provide the ability to build an income stream without your having to lock in a start date, and you can even decide not to exercise the income option.

On the other hand, there are real benefits to buying annuity income throughout retirement. The primary argument for deferring the purchase of income is that your health status may change, and deferring allows you to maintain liquidity and flexibility. Buying income over time allows for building an income stream without locking in with too high a percentage of assets. Annuity income generally becomes less expensive with age as payments are expected to be made for a shorter period of time, so deferring retains flexibility and allows for purchases at a reduced cost. Annuity income prices vary with interest rates, and buying income over time allows for protection from buying all the income at a time when interest rates are low and the income cost is too high. This is sometimes referred to as timing risk. As such, you should consider buying any product or investment over time instead of buying everything at once. By buying over time, you reduce the risk of buying at a bad time. With investments, this strategy is often referred to as dollar-cost averaging, but it can be used with other financial products like annuities as well.

In addition to these factors, there are some other factors relevant to the timing of a purchase. If the market has been up, purchasing income allows for locking in gains in the market. If medical advances extend life expectancy, the cost of income will increase. While buying an annuity is not for everyone, there are clear benefits when setting up a retirement income plan.

Hiring a financial advisor can really help with excess withdrawal risk and help you to pick the right type of annuity for your retirement plan. By placing some boundaries and a third party between you and your retirement assets, you can also help protect your assets from rash decisions and excess spending. People often see the stock market drop in value and immediately try to sell their investments, locking in losses. However, the best strategy is to ride out the storm in most cases. A good advisor can help you maintain the value of your assets and keep your income flowing. Additionally, the advisor can help you manage the sustainability of your plan over time and let you know whether you need to change your spending habits.

Be careful when helping out your family members. While you may want to help your children, if you give away too much, you might jeopardize your own retirement. This could also create an expectation from your children that you will always provide for them.

Lastly, beware of buying things like a boat or vacation home. Such purchases involve costs that go well beyond the original price tag. These items could create phantom expenses for the remainder of your retirement years, taking away assets that you need for more important things like health care. Ultimately, just make sure your expenses fit your retirement plan and budget. Don't overspend—make sure you know what you can spend! Determine a reasonable withdrawal rate at the beginning of your plan, budget for expenses (including family gifts), and stick to the plan throughout retirement.

HEALTH CARE EXPENSES

Medicare and Social Security have created the healthiest and most financially secure generation of senior citizens in American history.

—JIM WALSH, POLITICIAN

One of your biggest expenses in retirement will be health care–related costs. Out-of-pocket costs for health care for an average sixty-five-year old couple are often in the hundreds of thousands of dollars in retirement. Most people think they will need far less money saved up for health care because of Medicare. While Medicare is an incredible insurance program for retirees, it is not without its issues. For instance, Medicare has deductibles, co-pays, coverage limits, and no cap on out-of-pocket expenses, meaning you could spend $100,000 in a year on medical expenses. For most people, the biggest planning issue is just not realizing that Medicare requires some annual planning and review throughout retirement.

If you have employer-sponsored retirement health insurance coverage, it can go a long way in helping you meet your health care needs. If you can get retiree health care coverage from your former employer, you should look into it and see how it works with Medicare; however, such coverage is decreasing and is no longer common. Instead, once you hit age sixty-five, you will likely be eligible for Medicare Part A as long as you worked for ten years and are eligible for Social Security. However, you will still need to choose the appropriate insurance for yourself and your spouse as there are other areas of Medicare that are not automatic. This means you need to understand your options under Medicare and how the insurance helps you meet your specific health care needs.

For most people, Medicare coverage ends up consisting of a few major decisions. Medicare Part A primarily covers hospital bills and is paid for during your years of employment. There are no additional premiums for Part A when you retire as long as you are eligible for coverage. If you are not eligible for Part A, you can still pay annual premiums and get coverage. However, Medicare Part B—designed to cover doctor bills—does have a monthly premium. When signing up for Part B, there is an initial enrollment period. This period starts three months before your sixty-fifth birthday and continues for three months after, for a total of seven months. However, if you miss this window, you will have to wait until the next general enrollment period—January 1 to March 31—and your coverage won't start until the next July 1. Missing this enrollment period will also cause you to have a higher premium and a gap in insurance coverage.

Rewirement Alert

Many people do not realize that if you miss your Medicare enrollment period, you can be without insurance and be subject to penalty fees. Missing your open enrollment period can also cause any existing insurance you may have through COBRA or work to become secondary and not pay out.

In addition, you will need to decide whether you want to pay for Medicare Part D, which provides coverage for prescription drugs. When picking a Medicare Part D plan, you can choose from a variety of private plans in your area. Be sure to look at the premiums and what is covered under each plan. A plan with higher premiums may be more expensive, but it may also offer far more comprehensive coverage. One planning point in selecting a Medicare Part D plan is to talk to your local pharmacy. Find out what plans they see used in your area, what plans are easy to work with, and what plans would best cover the prescription drugs you need. Buy based on total benefits and not just on price!

Be aware of Medicare coverage gaps. There are co-pays, deductibles, and the dreaded Part D "donut hole," for which you are required to pay the full amount of your prescription drug costs for a period of time. While the Part D "donut hole" coverage gap is being reduced in the next few years, it will still exist and could cost you thousands of dollars.

Rewirement Alert

Many people do not realize that certain Medicare decisions require annual review. For instance, if you have Part D coverage for drugs, you should pay close attention to your plan each year and switch during the open enrollment period if your plan stops covering or increases the costs of the drugs you need.

In addition to getting Medicare Parts A, B, and D, you may want to consider a Medigap insurance policy to supplement your Medicare coverage. Medigap, or Medicare Supplement Insurance, can help to fill the gaps in coverage that exist in traditional Medicare. While the policies sold have to cover standard benefits, the premiums can vary from company to company. This means it's important to shop around. One company in your area could offer the exact same benefits and coverage as another company but charge a much higher premium.

If you still have time before retirement, consider taking advantage of a high-deductible health care plan. Having a high-deductible health care plan can allow you to save money in a health savings account (HSA). The HSA can be a very tax-efficient way to fund your health care costs because contributions are tax-free and withdrawals are tax-free as long as they are used for qualified health care expenditures. In 2017, you could contribute $3,400 (indexed number) for an individual with self-coverage and $6,750 (indexed number) for family coverage to an HSA. These limits are indexed annually to reflect cost-of-living changes. HSA funds can be used to help pay for Medicare premiums, long-term care premiums, and out-of-pocket expenses.

Fund a health savings account (HSA) if you are still working and have a high-deductible plan. This can lower your taxes for this year and give you a tax-deferred savings option to help you meet your retirement health care costs. For young individuals, use an HSA as a savings vehicle. Think about it as a retirement health care account. With the tax-free investment growth and tax deductibility of contributions, there is almost nothing better in the entire US savings system than an HSA. However, watch out for HSA fees, and pick a high-growth investment option if possible.

Planning for health care costs in retirement doesn't just start at age sixty-five when you are deciding on Medicare. Instead, it is a lifelong planning opportunity to make sure you have the right insurance leading up to Medicare, to put aside money for out-of-pocket costs, and to understand your Medicare benefits when it is time to enroll.

LONG-TERM CARE EXPENDITURES

Aging is out of your control. How you handle it, though, is in your hands.

—DIANE VON FURSTENBERG, FASHION DESIGNER

Too many people think that long-term care planning is just a decision about whether or not to purchase long-term care insurance. Long-term care planning, however, is so much more. It is a discussion about how you will fund this expense, where you will receive long-term care, and who will provide the care. Unfortunately, very few people are prepared to deal with this risk, as less than 8 percent of people have long-term care insurance and only 10 percent of people in the United States have a long-term care plan in place. This lack of planning is extremely troubling because long-term care is a very real and expensive risk. It is estimated that nearly 70 percent of people will need long-term care at some point. The average annual cost of a private nursing home room is roughly $100,000, showing 20 percent increases in cost over the past five years. On the high end, a private nursing home room can actually run over $200,000 annually. The cost of one year in a semiprivate nursing home room can easily exceed $150,000. With the cost of long-term care services rising, low long-term care insurance coverage, and few formal plans in existence, consideration of new options for funding long-term care expenses needs to be highlighted.

Long-term care planning can be done early in life, directly before retirement, and in some cases, during retirement. Ideally, it should be done before care is needed. In many cases, the best time to begin planning for long-term care as part of your overall retirement plan is when you are in your fifties and early sixties. Long-term care insurance becomes significantly more difficult to acquire in your late sixties and seventies.

Financing long-term care expenditures can be done through the purchase of long-term care insurance, which is specifically designed to cover such costs.

However, even insurance is not always a complete solution for financing these expenses. In some cases, it may be too expensive, not available, or just not right for the individual client. However, individuals will need to consider how much long-term care risk they want to pass on to an insurance company and how much they want to self-insure or rely upon the government. Long-term care insurance can be used to defray long-term care expenditures or provide almost-comprehensive coverage. As such, it is important that clients understand they can purchase insurance to cover just a portion of their projected expenses if they believe higher levels of long-term care insurance coverage are too expensive.

Rewirement Alert

Many people have the misconception that Medicare pays for long-term care expenses; it does not. But if you don't have a lot of money saved for retirement, Medicaid may be your best long-term care financing option. Otherwise, consider getting insurance.

Remember that if you want to purchase long-term care insurance, you should consider doing it in your forties and early fifties as part of your overall retirement plan. Long-term care insurance becomes significantly more difficult to acquire later in life, and many people are denied coverage by insurance companies at that point. Purchasing a long-term care insurance policy earlier in life can have the added benefit of locking in lower premiums.

While long-term care insurance is one way to fund long-term care expenses, it is not the only option. Policies can be expensive, can be unavailable to those who are not healthy enough to purchase them, and can often be considered objectionable due to their use-it-or-lose-it nature. Long-term care expenses can also be financed through a variety of newly developed hybrid or linked benefit products. One such product seeing tremendous growth and adoption is the life insurance policy that offers a tax-qualified long-term care rider. In fact, the sale of life insurance policies with long-term care riders has increased dramatically over the past few years. These hybrid life insurance and long-term care policies give the policy owner access to the majority of the death benefit if long-term care services are needed. If long-term care services are not needed, or if not all the death benefit is used up to pay for long-term care expenditures, the remaining death benefit is paid out to the beneficiaries upon the death of the policy owner.

Life insurance policies can also be used to fund long-term care costs in a variety of other manners. First, if the policy has a cash value, this amount can be accessed through withdrawals or policy loans to pay for long-term care expenses. Second, the policy could be sold (referred to as a life settlement option) to help pay for long-term care expenses. In some cases, a life settlement can give the policy owner up to three times the amount of money as the cash value option. A third option is a viatical settlement, which also involves selling the policy but is done when the policy owner is terminally ill. With this approach, proceeds from the sale are generally income tax–free. The sale price of the policy is determined by the future life expectancy of the terminally ill policy owner and the policy benefits.

In addition to life insurance and long-term care insurance hybrid policies, annuities have been linked to long-term care benefits. For example, some annuities now offer tax-qualified long-term care benefits. Companies like OneAmerica offer fixed annuities with long-term care riders, which enable you to invest the money you may have saved for long-term care in a product that provides a fixed income but will also provide higher payouts if you need long-term care benefits. In some cases, these types of products will double or triple the annuity payment when long-term care is needed. Additionally, hybrid products can be and usually are purchased with a single lump-sum payment. This can be an attractive feature for someone who does not prefer to pay annual or monthly long-term care insurance premiums that can rise significantly over time (which has occurred with some policies over the past few years). While most long-term care insurance policies try to keep premiums level, they can change and in some cases have doubled in cost. As such, some people like the certainty of a single-pay option because they have thereby reduced the risk of rising premium rates in the future. Lastly, both life insurance and annuity hybrid products solve the use-it-or-lose-it problem with long-term care insurance. If the long-term care benefit is not needed, benefits are available for other purposes.

If you own an existing life insurance or annuity product, you may be able to exchange that policy for a hybrid product that offers a long-term care benefit or for a stand-alone long-term care insurance policy. The Pension Protection Act of 2006 allowed for Section 1035 exchanges of traditional life insurance and annuity products for hybrid long-term care policies. For example, the life insurance policy could be Section 1035 exchanged tax-free for a long-term care insurance policy, despite the buildup of value inside the life insurance policy. Ultimately, like-kind exchanges under Section 1035 eliminate the taxable gain inside the annuity or life insurance policy because the qualified long-term care insurance policy allows for tax-free payouts for qualified expenses. If you have an outstanding life insurance policy, consider exchanging it tax-free for a hybrid life insurance and long-term care policy. This new policy can do double duty for you, and you can take advantage of some of the value built up in your old policy to help you reduce your long-term care risk.

Before purchasing either a life insurance or annuity long-term care hybrid product, it is crucial that you shop around as products and prices vary considerably. Also, make sure you are buying the product that best fits your needs and goals since not every product will work for every person and situation. Additionally, ensure that you can afford the investment before you make the purchase as some products do not offer any return of premiums and the decision will be final. Each person's situation is different, and you need to see whether any of these solutions fit your situation.

Another potential funding source for long-term care expenditures is a traditional income annuity. Income annuities have the advantage of paying out income whether long-term care is needed or not. Life annuity income can be purchased over time during retirement for you to build an income source later on when long-term care needs are likely to occur. The advantage of buying annuities over time is that you do not have to lock into the strategy entirely if your health or economic status changes. Another option is the deferred income annuity, in which you purchase a specified monthly annuity amount at a younger age (in your fifties or sixties) with the intention of beginning benefits later in retirement (ages eighty through eighty-five). This type of annuity can provide significant income at a relatively low cost because of the extended deferral period and the fact that annuities that begin later in your life have a much higher payout rate due to the shorter payout period.

Reverse mortgages can provide another option to pay for long-term care expenses. Reverse mortgages can pay out in the form of a lump-sum benefit, monthly payment, or a line of credit. The loan does not have to be repaid until the last homeowner borrower leaves the home. As such, a reverse mortgage does not necessarily help someone who ends up in a nursing home as the home will likely need to be sold to pay off the reverse mortgage. However, if an individual needs long-term care services in the home, a line of credit reverse mortgage may be an appropriate way for him or her to pay for this care and remain in the home.

While self-funding long-term care insurance, Medicaid, and family-provided care will all continue to be primary sources of long-term care funding for the foreseeable future, the market is changing, and more people are becoming aware of new and alternative solutions they can use to pay for long-term care. Whatever avenue you decide to take, having a plan in place is crucial. Even if you plan to rely on Medicaid, you will still need to spend down your assets before you can qualify. Furthermore, as new financing opportunities develop and your circumstances change, your long-term care plan will likely need continued monitoring and adjusting.

FRAILTY AND OLD AGE

Cherish all your happy moments; they make a fine cushion for old age.

—BOOTH TARKINGTON, AUTHOR

Aging brings with it a variety of retirement risks, including escalating health care expenses and possible long-term care expenses. While these represent significant financial risks for aging retirees, there is another risk, one often misunderstood and overlooked, lurking in the shadows—frailty risk. Frailty risk can pack a powerful punch on the security of your retirement plan and open you up to the risk of elder abuse. Really, this is just an unpleasant topic for people to talk about. That is the biggest hurdle here. Many people don't plan for incapacity and frailty because they simply do not want to address the elephant in the room. We all get older. This is a part of life.

Too often, people lump frailty risk in with long-term care and health care concerns. However, frailty risk results from deteriorating mental or physical health, creating a variety of issues for the retiree. These include financial problems, planning challenges, lifestyle changes, and additional threats to physical health. Frailty is not always easily defined but can loosely be characterized as that gradual loss of energy, strength, physical capability, and mental sharpness often associated with aging. Frailty is not simply aging, though it is highly correlated with aging. A University of Michigan study shows that nearly one-third of people age sixty-five and older suffer from some degree of frailty. While many people manage to remain active throughout retirement, many others go through different phases of activity, and activity decreases over time due to frailty issues. Frailty can spell unanticipated financial risk to a retirement plan.

An individual suffering from frailty during retirement may face significantly higher expenses. As you grow older and continue to live in place, the family home—once a crowded four-bedroom house full of children—becomes a large burdensome property to maintain. Each weekend, you clean, mow the grass, plant flowers, and perform other maintenance chores such as cleaning the gutters to keep your home up and running. However, as you age, you may not be able to get out the ladder, climb up onto the roof, and clean the gutters. Maybe it will cost you only a few hundred dollars a year to get a company to do it for you. The next year, you may no longer be able to mow the lawn every week or shovel the snow during the winter. Again, another few hundred dollars will be needed to hire someone to perform yard work. As frailty risk sets in, more and more home, personal, and other tasks become financial strains as you need to hire someone else to do it, rely on others for help, or forgo the tasks. If these maintenance jobs are left undone, your property could diminish in value and no longer be the financial asset you were counting on tapping into later in retirement.

At some point, frailty might become an even costlier issue if you are no longer able to drive. If you live in an area that requires driving due to a lack of good public transportation, this can represent a significant challenge and additional financial strain. The cost of hiring private drivers or taxicabs may be prohibitive, seriously curtailing an otherwise active and health-conscious lifestyle and further compounding the frailty factor. It should come as no surprise that in some cases, frailty has been shown to decrease one's ability to remain independent in retirement.

In addition to living independently, you may decide you want to purchase a new life insurance policy or obtain long-term care insurance coverage. However, the onset of frailty could be a factor in the underwriting process, possibly prohibiting you from being insurable. In some cases, you may be insurable but only at a much higher cost. This is a good reason to purchase long-term care insurance and life insurance at an early age, preferably in your fifties when the likelihood of being uninsurable is much lower.

Frailty will also impact other retirement income risks such as long-term care and health care costs. For example, research out of the University of Arizona shows that those suffering from frailty are more likely to have more severe injuries and develop complications when receiving treatment in the hospital. Furthermore, the research suggests that patients suffering from frailty experience both longer intensive care unit stays and longer overall lengths of stay in the hospital. The increased severity of injuries, additional complications, and extended stays in the hospital all add up to increased health care costs as a result of frailty.

Frailty does not have to ruin your retirement. In fact, proactive steps can be taken in order to reduce the risk of frailty and its potential impact on your retirement. Not all people suffer from frailty as they age. As a planning point, if you keep working even part time and stay active in retirement, you can hold off frailty and age-related diseases like Alzheimer's. Retiring early can have a detrimental impact on both your retirement savings and your health. As such, maintaining job skills, avoiding burnout, reducing work hours, and taking other measures can help to keep you in the workforce longer, decreasing the risk of frailty.

In addition to working longer, some other steps can be taken to minimize the likelihood of suffering frailty risk. Planning ahead of time is very important. For instance, setting up a trust and a trustee to make decisions for you can be a good way to deal with the decline in mental ability over time due to frailty. Planning ahead for the additional costs that result from frailty in maintaining a home, paying for health care, affording long-term care, and facilitating travel are also important. Downsizing early on in retirement or moving to a continuing care community to reduce the physical demands of homeownership can also be a good idea. Hiring others to maintain your home and perform tasks can be done but should be done with caution. There is an increased danger of financial elder abuse as more outsiders are introduced into the frail individual's life at the time when he or she may be most vulnerable. Lastly, taking the necessary steps to stay healthy and active as long as possible can help to reduce the likelihood and impact of frailty and all the financial risks that come with it.

As I discussed earlier, declining mental competency and physical capabilities can also open you up to the risk of physical, emotional, and financial elder abuse. Financial elder abuse is a huge risk and often goes unreported. However, it is estimated that the financial cost of elder abuse in the United States is in the billions of dollars every year. Often, financial elder abuse is accompanied by emotional abuse. Perhaps the most upsetting part is that it is typically family members, friends, and caregivers who engage in elder abuse. This can spoil a retiree's happiness and overall experience of retirement, even if the financial loss does not ruin his or her plan. Putting a third party in the way of your money can be a good way to protect against financial elder abuse. Establishing an intermediary, such as a financial advisor or an independent trustee, could help to protect your money against theft and misuse due to financial elder abuse.

Consider setting up a special power of attorney called a durable springing power of attorney, a health care power of attorney, and a living will to help you manage end-of-life issues such as incompetency. These legal documents can ensure that you get the care and quality of life you want later in retirement. An estate planning attorney can help you coordinate these with your overall retirement and estate plan.

STOCK MARKET RISKS

"Fasten your seatbelts, it's going to be a bumpy night."

—BETTE DAVIS, ACTRESS IN *ALL ABOUT EVE*

Stock market investments are volatile. The unpredictable ups and downs of the market are part of the investing experience. However, volatility is not always a bad thing. In fact, volatility usually indicates that stocks are ready for growth. But, you need to be able to resist the temptation to sell stocks when they take a dive and only buy when stocks are up. Buy low, sell high. That is the investor's best friend and motto. Unfortunately, few individual investors end up following this guide.

The reality is that part of your retirement income plan will likely include a significant amount of stock market investments due to their long-term growth potential. Typically, higher-risk investments tend to offer higher rates of return. This is essentially a trade-off between certainty and uncertainty. But remember that all types of investments come with certain risks, not just stocks. For instance, bonds and other guaranteed-income sources often suffer from liquidity issues, and their returns can be outpaced by inflation. Additionally, even bond and annuity payments could falter under the right catastrophic conditions.

When investing in stocks, there is a degree of uncertainty as the average growth has historically varied a lot in the United States. Even though there is a risk that you could suffer a financial loss in the market, research shows that most people need to be invested in the market to help their portfolio sustainability. Investing in stocks can also help with inflation as stock prices and dividends tend to adjust somewhat for inflation over time, allowing you to maintain your purchasing power throughout retirement.

Instead of avoiding the market completely, you just need to be smart about investing. This means using dollar-cost averaging, diversifying investments, and holding stocks for long periods of time. First, avoid purchasing all your investments in one day. Instead, buy stocks over time and give them plenty of time to grow. This also means resisting the urge to overreact when the market has a bad week and selling your stocks at a loss. Be patient, and ride out down parts of the market. Try to overcome those detrimental behavioral biases that drive people to buy high and sell low.

Rewirement Alert

Don't leave the stock market entirely when you retire. While stocks are volatile and carry some risk, they also provide excellent returns in the long run to help fund a lengthy retirement.

Second, make sure you are diversifying your investments between asset classes, such as stocks versus bonds, and within asset classes. This means you shouldn't own too much of any one company as a long-term investment strategy. You need to acknowledge the risk that one company's stock is very volatile over time. It is better to buy a lot of unrelated company stocks to help reduce volatility. However, remember that if you are invested in the market, you cannot completely avoid market risk, even when properly diversified. When the market drops, it drops.

To reduce investment risks early in retirement, consider a collar strategy to hedge your investments during the first few years. A collar is an options trading hedge that is created by buying protective puts (protection against the stock's falling too low) by selling a call option (which gives someone else the ability to buy the stock if the stock goes up a lot) on shares of stock you already own. It costs you nothing out of pocket and limits your upside and downside. It can be effective for a few years in early retirement but should not last the entire time—it will severely impact your long-term gains, as it is a hedging technique against risk.

When picking your investments, it is also important to take a look at the liquidity of your investment. This is really a measure of how fast you can turn an investment into cash. For example, real estate or business ownership investments may seem like a good opportunity, but if you cannot easily sell the property or business interest for years, the lack of liquidity needs to be considered. Stocks tend to have a lot of liquidity as you can often sell them within days. When discussing liquidity, look at your overall plan and be aware of assets that can be quickly turned into cash to meet expenditures. The stock market and investments are your friends. Be smart and don't panic—your investments are crucial to the success of your retirement plan.

UNEXPECTED EARLY RETIREMENT

If you change the way you look at things, the things you look at change.

—WAYNE DYER, PHILOSOPHER

While you will have some control over the time at which and manner in which you leave the workforce, many people are forced into retirement earlier than they expected. Nearly 45 percent of retirees say they retired earlier than expected, approximately 45 percent say they retired when they planned to, and 10 percent say they retired later than planned. For those who retired early, declining health was the primary reason why. This will be one area that may be hard to fully control. However, leading a healthy and active lifestyle can help you remain fit enough to continue working and retire on your own terms.

The second most cited reason for early retirement is to fulfill family care-giving responsibilities, whether it is to care for elderly parents or a spouse. These responsibilities often fall on full-time working women and can create emotional, physical, mental, and financial issues for the caregiver, even impacting his or her own health and career. So how can you manage this risk? First, talk to your parents and family about having a long-term care plan in place. If they have a plan, all the burden might not fall on you. Additionally, you can limit the impact on your spouse and children by having a long-term care plan in place for yourself. Long-term care planning is not just a financial decision; it is about protecting the family unit. In fact, you can even consider purchasing long-term care insurance for your parents or at least having a discussion with them about their long-term care plans. A well-designed long-term care plan can have a tremendously positive impact on your other family members because they will not have to bear the full responsibility of funding and providing your care. Purchasing long-term care insurance for a parent or spouse can improve his or her retirement security and your own by reducing the caretaker burden on yourself. If not for both spouses, consider purchasing long-term care insurance for the female spouse only as she will likely need care for a longer period of time.

Rewirement Alert

Many people fall into an anchor point trap and retire too early. Don't worry about when your friends or relatives retired. Instead, pick a retirement date that works for you. Age sixty-two (or sixty-five) is not a magic retirement number. Ignore those numbers and figure out what works in your situation.

The third most cited reason for forced early retirement is corporate downsizing. Losing a job just a few years before you were planning to retire could severely impact your retirement security in a variety of ways. You may have to start spending your retirement assets earlier than expected; you will be subject to inflation for a longer period of time; you will most likely have a reduced rate of savings; and you may have to collect Social Security earlier than anticipated. In order to avoid these situations, you need to keep yourself employable until you choose to retire. This means staying engaged at work, continuing to develop your marketable skills, keeping up with continued education, and maintaining your professional networks. All of these are really investments in yourself. Spending the time and money to continue your professional growth, even into your midsixties, can provide a lot of value since you can better control your retirement and your future security. These activities are investments in your human capital or lifetime earning potential. Continue to invest in yourself so you can maintain employment and find reemployment, if necessary, to ensure that you can retire on your own terms.

Early retirement means a longer retirement period, which means you will need more money. Many people who retire early feel the need to collect Social Security before their full retirement age. If your full retirement age is sixty-seven and you begin to collect benefits at age sixty-two, those benefits will be permanently reduced by 30 percent. Remember that when you retire and when you start to collect Social Security benefits can be two separate decisions. Even if you are laid off from work before you can retire, you can still delay taking your Social Security benefits by using other assets first. By delaying Social Security benefits, you can help protect your retirement security.

Consider delaying Social Security benefits for as long as possible to increase your retirement security. In some cases, you may need to use up other assets like your 401(k) or personal savings first in order to defer Social Security benefits. Delaying Social Security until age seventy will result in annual payments that are 76 percent higher than they would have been had you started collecting at age sixty-two.

Early retirement may also force you to tap into your 401(k) or pension early. If you have a defined benefit pension plan, you can usually start collecting benefits as early as age sixty-two without suffering a reduction in benefits. If this is the case, it may make a lot of sense to take advantage of the early retirement and turn on the defined benefit plan. However, in some cases, you may have to wait until age sixty-five for the benefits to begin. When retiring from your company, take a serious look at the distribution options that are being offered. Make sure you look at the differences between the annuity option and the lump-sum option. An annuity option may be the best choice for your specific situation, especially if you have a spouse who might need future income.

When leaving your job, make sure you examine your 401(k) and pension plan distribution options. A lump sum may seem preferable as you will have control of your money, but the annuity option offered in your plan may be better than anything you can purchase on the open market for the same cost. Individuals with guaranteed sources of income, like a pension, also tend to be happier in retirement as they have more peace of mind about their income.

If you do decide to take a lump-sum distribution, make sure you roll over the lump sum into an IRA or other qualified plan. Consider doing a direct rollover or transfer to an IRA so that your previous employer does not have to withhold a 30 percent mandatory tax from your 401(k). This will help you get the full 401(k) account balance into your IRA and allow it to continue to grow until you need to take a distribution. The IRA rollover decision is an important one for your retirement. Make sure to find a knowledgeable advisor or specialist who can help you with your rollover decisions and guide your subsequent investment strategies. Pay attention to the fees in the investments you roll over and understand how your advisor or IRA rollover specialist gets compensated.

When rolling your 401(k) or other qualified plan over to an IRA, make sure you know whether you have any employer stock inside your 401(k) that could be eligible for special tax treatment as net unrealized appreciation. If you do have employer stock in your 401(k), you will want to consider doing an in-kind distribution. This would mean taking the stock out of the 401(k) and not rolling it into an IRA but holding it as a taxable account instead. You will also need to distribute your entire remaining 401(k) balance within the year, or you will lose the special tax treatment. The employer stock will be taxed as ordinary income and as a distribution in the current year up to the amount that you invested, essentially your cost basis in the stock. Any additional growth in the employer stock from when it was in your 401(k) can then be taxed as long-term capital gains instead of ordinary income when you decide to sell the employer stock. Long-term capital gains rates, usually 15 percent, tend to be much lower for individuals than their ordinary income tax rates. As such, correctly managing your distribution and employer stock can save you hundreds of thousands of dollars if you invested heavily in your employer's stock.

Early retirement can create a lot of unique challenges, but if you prepare properly, you can retire on your own terms. Furthermore, early retirement does not mean you have to make bad financial decisions. You can still defer Social Security benefits, take the right distribution from your employer retirement plan, and roll over assets into an IRA. Lastly, don't forget to continue to invest in yourself. This can keep you employable late into life, improve your lifetime earning potential, and allow you to minimize the risk of forced early retirement.

UNEXPECTED FINANCIAL RESPONSIBILITY

The man who complains about the way the ball bounces is likely to be the one who dropped it.

—LOU HOLTZ, FOOTBALL COACH

Another roadblock to a secure retirement can be unexpected expenses. These can come in a variety of forms. You could get in a car accident or get sick, your house could burn down or flood, you could lose a spouse earlier than expected, or you could suddenly discover that you have to support a family member. When planning for retirement, it is important that you have the right insurance protection to avoid potential setbacks. This means having the right amount of property and casualty insurance (through good auto and home coverage) to protect you and your family. Consider getting more auto coverage than the state required minimums, as these often do not protect you properly against liability. Being underinsured could threaten your retirement savings.

A car accident or sickness could easily ruin your retirement savings and security if you are not properly prepared. This is why it is necessary to have the correct amount of disability and health insurance coverage. If your employer does offer them, consider signing up through work, as your company is likely paying part of the costs. However, if your employer does not offer health or disability insurance, you can still purchase the insurance on the open market.

The early loss of a spouse can have a huge impact on your retirement income security, overall plans, and happiness. Honestly, the last thing you want to be thinking about when you lose a life partner is whether you will be financially secure in retirement. Make sure you have the proper amount of life insurance to protect against this risk. Life insurance can be a valuable retirement income asset. It can help to protect the family unit during working years and into retirement. Whole life policies with cash value can also provide a source of income as the cash value can be accessed in retirement. Additionally, life insurance is one of the few ways to generate millions of dollars as a legacy in an estate.

Life insurance should be purchased for both working and nonworking spouses. One of the largest underinsured populations in the country is that of the nonworking or part-time working spouse. This spouse adds a lot of value to the household, and this person's loss would put a huge financial burden on the surviving spouse. Don't get caught unprepared. Get adequate life insurance to help protect your family and your retirement income security. One way to think about life insurance is that it is sold in two different forms, temporary life insurance or permanent life insurance. A simple way to put it is that temporary life insurance (term) is more about protecting families, and permanent life insurance is more about wealth accumulation and legacy planning. Term is typically the more affordable policy.

Some people think that life insurance is about only your working years. However, it is also about protecting income streams. In retirement, you are still a source of income. For instance, when a spouse dies in retirement, Social Security will pay the surviving spouse the higher of the two spouses' benefits. However, the lower benefit will be gone. In some cases, this can cut your retirement income almost in half, even if you still have nearly 80 percent of the expenses you had before. Life insurance can help to protect against the lost Social Security income from the death of a spouse.

Rewirement Alert

Life insurance should not be underestimated as a retirement income planning tool. The right policy can protect the family unit, provide income streams to make up for lost Social Security benefits, and provide a legacy amount for your heirs.

You can also suffer a financial burden by gaining a family member instead of losing one. Perhaps a parent, sibling, or child moves (back) into your home. This can become a serious financial burden and can often be unexpected. If your child moves back in, make sure you are still fostering a home that supports financial independence. You need to take care of yourself and cannot sacrifice your retirement security to fund your children's lifestyles. Make sure you set goals and clear parameters; don't let them become reliant on your finances. Helping a child or family member can feel like an obligation and be the right thing to do for you, but make sure you do it the right way. Don't allow yourself to be taken advantage of financially, and make sure you are encouraging sound financial behavior. This can help you minimize the financial impact on your own savings and still support your family.

4

Putting a Retirement Plan Into Play

WHEN TO BEGIN RETIREMENT INCOME PLANNING

It does not do to leave a live dragon out of your calculations, if you live near him.

—J. R. R. TOLKEIN, AUTHOR

Once you understand the risks you face in retirement, you can develop a comprehensive plan to deal with them. However, at some point, you will need to prioritize your risks. This will require setting out goals, reviewing your personal finances, and examining your sources of retirement income. Depending on your unique situation and goals, certain risks may require more attention than others. For instance, if you are single, you will be less concerned about providing care to other family members. However, you may be more concerned about your own long-term care risk as you won't be able to rely upon a spouse to provide the care.

Remember that you really cannot properly prioritize your risks until you take a comprehensive look at your retirement income plan and situation. If you worked for a company that provides a large defined benefit pension plan with cost-of-living adjustments, you will be less worried about longevity and inflation risk. However, if you want to leave a large legacy, this may change your plan and compel you to invest your other assets in higher-risk investments to increase the likelihood of higher returns.

Also, when engaging in comprehensive retirement planning, you may solve one risk while exacerbating another one. For example, if you deal with longevity risk by purchasing a single premium immediate life annuity, you have likely increased your liquidity risk. Again, because you have limited assets to meet your retirement income needs, you will need to prioritize your goals and risks. An advisor who specializes in retirement income can help you build a plan to meet your unique situation. There are also software programs available to help you prioritize your retirement goals and risks, such as LIMRA's Ready-2-Retire. Additionally, nonprofit mission-driven organizations like the American College of Financial Services and the Society of Actuaries both provide free information on retirement income planning and postretirement risks.

While risks and roadblocks to a successful retirement are around every corner, a well-defined retirement income plan can help you reduce these risks and improve your financial security. Remember that you don't need to save more money to deal with all these risks. Instead, you can limit the impact of many of these retirement risks by making well-informed and strategic decisions. Understand the risks you face, know what strategies are available, don't be afraid to ask for help, and be proactive. The biggest impediment to a more secure retirement is inaction. But most importantly, everyone can improve their retirement income security without saving a single dollar more simply by making better and more-informed decisions. So let's start looking at how to plan.

An important question is *When is it time to begin putting together a retirement income plan?* Since there is almost always something you can do to improve your retirement security, planning should begin when you are ready. Unfortunately, most don't begin to think about this stage of planning until they are about to retire and begin to confront retirement decisions—like when to retire or when to claim Social Security benefits. Others begin to plan even later, once they are in retirement and begin to question whether their resources will last a lifetime. If you start late, don't worry; there are still strategies in this book that will help you. Also, planning is required throughout retirement—so it's never too late to build a plan.

The best time to build your first comprehensive plan is five to ten years prior to retirement. Prior to that time, you may not have enough information about the details of your retirement to formulate a comprehensive plan. Many who are five to ten years from retirement have an established lifestyle with a relatively clear cost, a sense of when retirement may begin, and at least some feeling for the changes that retirement will bring. They will also have accumulated resources that can be used to fund retirement and are still far enough from retirement to make some changes if the planning process identifies that the current goals are not easily obtainable. Using a simple ten-step process can help you to build a plan to meet your needs. However, the plan should be revisited at least every year throughout retirement.

If you are further from retirement than this, good for you for planning early. There are still plenty of steps that you can take to better prepare yourself for retirement. Also, starting to think about income planning early will change the way you think about your retirement planning. When you think in terms of generating income versus simply building wealth, you pay attention to the costs of generating income.

It also starts to move the conversation to a life cycle investment approach wherein the goal is smoothing income from a time of working to a time when you are not working. Thinking in terms of income also expands the way we think about building retirement resources as buying rental property can mean steady income in retirement, and even the equity built with homeownership can be used in retirement.

Maybe the most critical issue when you still have many years before retirement is focusing on building retirement assets. For millennials and other young individuals, the focus should not yet be on retirement income planning but rather on wealth accumulation. Now, the real issue becomes how you can accumulate the appropriate amount of wealth in order to set yourself up for a financially secure future and retirement.

There are many other opportunities to plan for a financially secure future prior to retirement. Here are some ideas:

- Retirement security is affected by employment decisions as some companies have better pensions, retiree health care, and executive benefits. Take employer-sponsored benefits into consideration when looking at the overall compensation package.

- If you choose self-employment, your retirement could be adversely affected as the onus of planning will be placed solely on you.

- Once you have begun to build wealth, it is important to protect it. Having sufficient homeowner's insurance, liability coverage, life insurance, and disability insurance all go a long way in improving retirement security for you and your family. Remember to protect yourself. Your human capital, which is your ability to make a living, is the best way for you to build financial wealth over time. However, in retirement, when you stop working, your human capital is gone. At this point, you need to replace your human capital with financial savings and other retirement income sources.

- Purchase long-term care insurance when you are still healthy and able to afford it. Many consider age fifty the right time to look into this product—which provides protection if you become unable to care for yourself.

- If your employer does not have a defined benefit pension plan, well before retirement, you may want to consider looking into some guaranteed income, which will begin at retirement age. There are several types of annuity contracts that can be used to lock into a specified amount of income when you retire.

Now, even if you are decades away from retirement, you still need to be saving. Even in your twenties and thirties, you should be setting aside money for the future. It can feel very daunting during your early working years to set aside money into the company 401(k) plan or to set up an IRA. However, it is so important that you save early and often. It is also important that you save in a smart way. This means taking advantage of the tax benefits and any employer-provided benefits. For instance, if your employer offers a 401(k) match for your salary deferral, you should consider contributing at least enough to the 401(k) to get the employer match. However, if you have outstanding credit card bills that you are not paying, you may want to consider suspending any retirement savings until those credit cards are paid off and your budget is back on track.

Another thing to consider is whether or not a 401(k) is the best way for you to save early in your career. Traditional 401(k) salary deferrals allow you to contribute a portion of your income to the account and defer taxes into the future. The benefits of deferred taxes are quite substantial, even if tax rates rise in the future. However, if you are in a low tax bracket, a Roth IRA or Roth 401(k) salary deferral is likely much more beneficial in the long run. While the Roth contribution is taxed today, any gains in the investments will come out tax-free later on in your life if you meet certain Roth holding period require-ments for qualified distributions. So, if your employer does not offer a 401(k) match and you are early in your career, you may want to consider forgoing any savings in the 401(k) and instead set up a Roth IRA. Additionally, the Roth IRA has more flexibility with regard to taking withdrawals than an IRA or 401(k). For many people just getting started with their savings, it is a great relief to have some access to their savings in a Roth IRA without having to worry about the additional 10 percent early withdrawal penalty tax that accompanies most withdrawals from 401(k)s prior to age 59.5. In fact, this can actually encourage some to save more money because they know they have access to their contri-butions without incurring penalties.

One last tip relates to your investments at an early age. The simplest idea is that people in their twenties and thirties should be primarily invested in stocks or other high-earning investments. However, for your very first invest-ment, it does make sense to be a little more conservative. Behavioral finance shows that if you pick a super risky investment as your first investment and the value of that investment drops dramatically, like the 2008 stock market did, you could be driven away from making similar investments in the future. As such, it is best to ease your way into the stock market over the first few years of your savings. However, if you are comfortable with the ups and downs of the market, you can start off with more of your investments in equities.

If you just landed your first job, make sure you understand your employer-sponsored retirement plan. If it is a 401(k), find out whether there is a com-pany match, and consider deferring enough of your salary to get the match. However, after you get that company match, you may want to consider saving any other money in a Roth IRA if you are in a low tax bracket instead of putting additional savings into the 401(k).

Rewirement Alert

You cannot beat the company match. It is basically free money. Too many people still do not defer enough to get the full employer match in a 401(k). If you have this option, you should be taking advantage of it.

Now, once you have accumulated a significant amount of savings and start to near your retirement, the emphasis on accumulation planning will start to switch to decumulation or income planning. It is time for us to take all those assets you have saved and turn them into a reliable stream of income that can last throughout your retirement and meet your income needs.

BUILDING A RETIREMENT INCOME PLAN IN TEN STEPS

Give me six hours to chop down a tree and I will spend the first four sharpening the axe.

—ABRAHAM LINCOLN, PRESIDENT

Now that we have looked at many of the risks we face in retirement, we can start the process of putting together a plan. A retirement income plan needs to be comprehensive in nature, taking into account both financial and nonfinancial aspects of one's life. There is no way around the fact that retirement income planning is difficult. In order to generate a plan that will meet your retirement income needs, a broad range of factors must be considered. For instance, you will need to review your current situation, determine your retirement goals, estimate your retirement income needs, understand your Social Security options, manage your expenses, look at tax issues, and develop a plan to turn your assets into income that will meet your retirement objectives. A well-positioned and well-developed retirement income plan can improve your financial security without your needing to save another dime for retirement. There is real value in planning when it comes to retirement income.

While getting a plan set up is difficult because of the breadth and complexity of the issues that must be addressed, maintaining that plan over time may be even more difficult. Change is constant and will impact your retirement plan as your retirement may last thirty or more years. Pause for a minute and reflect on where you were thirty years ago. Are your desires still the same? Would a plan you set up decades ago work for you today? The answer is probably no. Take another look at how much the legal, tax, and financial landscapes have changed over the past thirty years. You cannot rely upon today's market and legal forces to remain constant for decades. Today, interest rates are low, people have undersaved for retirement, employer-sponsored pension plans are a rarity, and people are living longer than ever. However, it's unrealistic to expect these trends to be the same forever. Interest rates will rise, and the market and world will continue to evolve. So you need to be ready for changes and for your own future. Having a process in place to develop a retirement plan is crucial to your secure retirement. In this section, a ten-step retirement income plan is provided to help you review your own situation and get on the right path to a successful retirement.

STEP 1—EVALUATE YOUR CURRENT SITUATION

If you don't know where you are going, you'll end up someplace else.

—YOGI BERRA, HALL OF FAME BASEBALL PLAYER

In order to figure out where you are going, you first need to know where you are coming from. This means you need to take a full account of your financial situation as well as other emotional and personal factors. This information will be crucial in developing an effective retirement income plan. If you don't have good information upfront, the plan will not be successful. Putting garbage into the plan will only result in garbage coming out of the plan.

First, you will need to take a look at your family situation. Retirement planning is really goals-based planning. Most people structure their goals around their family obligations. You may have a large family in which many people depend on you as the breadwinner of the family unit. Sometimes you may be needed to provide emotional and other constructive support that is nonfinancial in nature. However, in other cases, you may be relied on financially to support a dependent adult child, a sibling, a parent, or another family member. This type of situation can create a real financial hurdle when planning for retirement.

Even if you do not have significant familial support obligations, you may find that your retirement happiness will, in part, be driven by spending time with your family. This could determine your living location in retirement and the manner in which you want to spend your time. Relocating to be closer to grandchildren or planning regular long-distance visits to family members may be part of your future. Additionally, strong family relationships often create a desire to leave a legacy amount behind once you pass away.

Besides caring for your children or parents, you also need to take a look at any support you may have to provide to a spouse, partner, or divorced spouse.

This can also create both financial and emotional hurdles for an individual. Do you still owe support to a former spouse? Will you have to support your current spouse or partner? Does he or she have any family members that you may have to support, individually or as a couple? While putting together a good overview of one's demographic data may not seem like the most important step, it is fundamental to envisioning your retirement and generating a comprehensive plan.

Next, you will have to spend some time thinking about yourself. Make a list of the activities you enjoy, the activities you would rather eliminate, the things that you consider important in your life, and the issues that keep you up at night. This personal inventory list will serve as a collection of qualitative information that can help you better understand what you need and want from a retirement income plan.

Finally, you need to put together a complete list of your financial assets and liabilities. Collecting this quantitative data is crucial to understanding your current financial situation. You cannot develop a path to a successful retirement income plan without knowing where your current resources stand. You will likely want to develop a balance sheet that represents all your assets and liabilities. There are a variety of free online balance sheet tools that can help you organize your assets and liabilities. You can even do this in a simple Excel file and keep it safely on your home computer. If you do not feel comfortable putting together all this information, you can go to a financial planner or your accountant to get help setting up a balance sheet.

When setting up a balance sheet, you will want to categorize your assets to get a better understanding of where your assets are and how available they are for use in retirement. For instance, figure out how much cash, or cash equivalents, you have. Cash equivalents are anything that can be readily turned into cash in just a few days. Next, you should look at your financial assets, which include amounts invested in stocks, bonds, mutual funds, and other investment vehicles. This would include amounts you have saved in your 401(k), IRA, health savings account (HSA), trust, or other investment management vehicles. These financial assets are not as readily available as they are more subject to timing restrictions and sensitive to market considerations. Another important asset category includes insurance products like life insurance, health insurance, disability insurance, long-term care insurance, and longevity annuities.

Next, consider any business interests you own. For example, you may own your own business or own part of a family business. This asset could have tremendous value but may require special planning in order for you to successfully monetize your business interest wealth. For many small business owners and family-owned businesses, it can be tremendously challenging to liquidate the business and realize the full value of the company.

After accounting for business interests, you need to account for any real property, such as your residence, land, vacation home, or investment property. These assets are not always listed as financial in nature because you often need a place to live, and so, you may not be in a position to monetize your home. For most people, their homes tend to be one of their largest assets, even though they do not always have easy access to that value as homes are a bit illiquid and cannot always be sold immediately for their full market value.

Lastly, you need to consider any tangible or intangible personal property you may own. Tangible property tends to include all those things you can pick up and move around, such as cars, jewelry, paintings, furniture, and so on. Intangible personal property items can be equally important and represent considerable value. A new type of intangible personal property is causing havoc for retirement and estate planning: digital assets. Do not overlook these special assets as they can cost you a great deal of money if not properly managed. Digital assets are not computers or cell phones but all those accounts that you have stored on your phone, on your computer, or online. This could include your bank, PayPal, Bitcoin, Amazon, e-mail, and Facebook accounts. Some of these accounts feel only sentimental in nature but can have tremendous value. Again, if you are operating a small business or blog, your online accounts could have a lot of financial value. Even if you do not generate money from your digital assets, failure to account for them and manage them over time could put you at risk of financial loss. For example, if one of the online accounts were hacked, your personal and financial information would be vulnerable. If you own a business, who would have access to the login information and manage those online accounts if you were suddenly unable to do this yourself? Digital assets have real value and need to be considered and properly managed over time.

After you have all your assets accounted for on the balance sheet, you need to start working on determining your liabilities, a task that may be even more painful than adding up your assets. No one likes to look at the debts he or she owes each and every day. The three most common types of liabilities are housing debt, student loan debt, and credit card debt. However, you could have other types of debt obligations, such as a business debt, an installment sale debt obligation, and unpaid utilities or medical bills.

In addition to listing your debt obligation, you should review the reason for the debt obligation. Was the money used to help you grow a business, was it used to help someone go to college, was it used to pay for an unexpected or uninsured medical event, or was it the result of poor money management? Also of importance is the payment schedule for each debt. Do you have monthly payments, yearly payments, or late charges to consider? Worth noting too are the interest rates that accompany these debt obligations. For instance, the interest rates on credit card debt are usually substantially higher than those on student loans. Credit card rates are going to be higher than what you can reasonably expect as an investment return from the stock market, so you may be better served by paying off high-rate debt as opposed to saving more money. However, until you take a look at all your debt, the reasons for the debt, their payment schedules, and the applicable interest rates, you will not know how to prioritize your payments.

Once you have set up a balance sheet of your assets and liabilities, you will be ready to create a cash flow statement that tracks your income and expenses for at least a month. Ideally you should track every dollar of income and every dollar of expense for a full year. Establishing your income is relatively easy as you have documentation for income sources, such as your employer-provided W-2s.

Tracking your expenses, on the other hand, can be more difficult. Your bank account and credit card statements can help you track this information. Some credit card companies and banks even offer a breakdown of your expenditures online as a free service. Find what services your bank and credit card company offer you at no charge. Take advantage of these services if they are available. Just seeing how much you spend on a given item in a year can help you reprioritize your goals and spending habits. I had a friend who, at the end of the year, checked her credit card statement, which was broken down into spending areas. She realized that she had spent over $3,000 that year on coffee alone! This was shocking to her. The five-dollar coffees didn't seem to cost her a lot at the time of each purchase, but over the course of the year, they cost her a tremendous amount of money. This information motivated her to reevaluate her spending habits and contribute more to her savings by brewing her own coffee. There are limited options available to increase your income each year aside from the raises you get from your employer. However, you do have much more control of the expense side of your life. A good cash flow statement can help you identify key spending areas and prioritize your spending accordingly.

Rewirement Alert

Don't forget to include the value of your home in your plan. Accounting for all your current assets and expenditures can help you prioritize spending cuts and areas for increased savings.

Action Steps: Gather Data

- Start by figuring out how you feel about your finances. How much do you value security of principal? How much do you value avoidance of fees? How much do you want to automate? How much do you want in liquid assets? Do you want inflation protection? Do you want high returns?

- Collect all your financial information. Having everything in one place will help you get started. It is also useful if you are going to seek help from a professional and is helpful to your family if something happens to you.
- Keep track of your spending. Pick a software tool that helps to make this process simple.
- Create a personal balance sheet and cash flow statement with the personal finance tool that you have chosen.

STEP 2—DETERMINE YOUR RETIREMENT GOALS

Setting goals is the first step in turning the invisible into the visible.

—TONY ROBBINS, LIFE COACH

The second step of the retirement income planning process requires envisioning your retirement. What do you want to be doing? Where do you want to be living? Do you want to have to worry about long-term care, your children, or a legacy goal? Envisioning your retirement is so important when setting out a retirement income plan. So many people never really take the time to think about what they want their retirement to be like. Instead, they just find themselves retired, struggling to meet their needs and searching for meaning. Furthermore, while you may envision one thing for your retirement, your spouse may envision something entirely different. You may also find out that you do not have the retirement assets to fund your desired retirement goals, forcing you to either revise your goals or somehow enhance your retirement savings.

It is often easier to envision the beginning of retirement than the later stages of retirement. First of all, the earlier retirement years, or the "go-go" years of retirement, are the closest in time and often represent an active lifestyle. It is during this retirement period that most people expect to travel, play golf, and experience the joys of retirement. As such, an increase in travel, activities, and spending must be accounted for in the plan.

Following the "go-go" years of retirement is a time marked by declining activity and health and other life limitations—the "slow-go" years. This period can still be incredibly rewarding and enjoyable. However, your expectations, planning, and financing need to adjust to a changing lifestyle.

It is the years following the "go-go" and "slow-go" years that people do not enjoy envisioning because doing so often puts them face-to-face with their own mortality, fears, and suffering. These are the "no-go" years, a time that requires comprehensive and thoughtful planning. Planning for the "no-go" stage is crucial because at that time, we may no longer be able to take care of ourselves independently, and we may no longer be able to make informed decisions. Instead, we will have to rely upon others and trust that we have managed our financial assets appropriately and will have sufficient income for the entirety of our lives. This time is often marked by decreased health to the point where travel and daily activities become challenging. Many people end up needing long-term care services as they are no longer able to care for themselves. This can be an incredibly expensive period, especially if long-term care services are needed or a catastrophic health care event occurs.

It is important to sit down and discuss your retirement goals with others. This is your life; make sure you live it the way you want to. Be honest and open with your spouse and family members about what you want to do, where you want to live, the people you want to spend time with, and how you want your care delivered if you cannot take care of yourself in the future. If you don't tell people what you want and you don't plan for it, no one else will. You will not be able to generate a well-defined retirement income plan without first defining the kind of retirement you want to live. Take the time to envision your retirement honestly and realistically. A great way to start is by asking yourself the following questions. If you are married, you and your spouse may want to do this exercise separately and then discuss the answers together.

Action Steps: Questions to Ask Yourself

- When do you think you want to retire?
- Where do you think you would like to live when you first retire?
- Does work factor into your idea of retirement?
- If you are going to work, will you continue with the same type of work or choose something different?
- Is continued work tied more to life meaning, filling your time, or needing the income?

- If you are not planning on working, what types of activities do you expect to provide meaning?
- Will you travel extensively in retirement to see new sites or visit friends or relatives?
- What recreational activities do you want to do?
- Do you have family members who rely on you, and if so, how does that impact your retirement?
- Do you want to go back to school?
- Do you want to volunteer?
- Who do you want to spend time with in retirement?
- Do you have any health issues that may impact your retirement lifestyle?
- How are you going to stay healthy?
- If you needed more help later in retirement, would you be likely to move again, possibly to be closer to family?
- If you needed more help later in retirement, how do you see yourself getting that help? Would you seek help from family and friends? Where would you get long-term care should the need arise?

STEP 3—ESTIMATE YOUR RETIREMENT INCOME NEEDS

By failing to prepare, you are preparing to fail.

—BENJAMIN FRANKLIN, INVENTOR

Now that you have looked at how much your life is costing and identified how retirement may be different, you will be able to estimate your retirement income needs. Essentially, this step is figuring out how large of a paycheck you will need each and every month to live your life according to your goals. There are a variety of ways to calculate your retirement income needs. If you are more than five years from retirement, the income replacement ratio method is the best one to use. This method takes your average gross salary for the past three years and multiplies that by something between 60 and 80 percent to give you an expected yearly income amount that you will need to meet your goals. This method assumes that you do not need 100 percent of your current income because you are no longer saving for retirement, will maintain the same standard of living, and will see some general lifestyle reductions in retirement. Most people experience lower tax rates in retirement because decreased taxable income, as a portion of Social Security benefits, is not subject to taxation and there is a higher standard deduction starting at age sixty-five. Other expenses related to employment, such as clothing and commuting costs, also tend to decrease. However, you could experience higher costs associated with increased travel and rising health care expenses. The largest reduction is usually attributed to a cessation in saving for retirement, which should free up about 10 percent of your income per year.

The income replacement ratio method can be a useful yardstick for predicting retirement needs during the years leading up to retirement. However, this method will fall short in predicting an accurate account of your retirement expenses. Luckily, there is a far better method once you near retirement: the adjusted expense method. With the adjusted expense method, you take all your annual expenses just before you retire and use that total as an estimate of your aggregate expenses for retirement. You need to account for all your expenses: housing, transportation, food, health, personal items, insurance, recreation, interest payments, entertainment, dining, travel, gifts, and charitable donations.

The adjusted expense method does need modifications based on your lifestyle, your finances, your retirement goals, and your current economic conditions. Remember too that your expenses should reduce a bit in retirement. However, this does not occur for everyone. Other adjustments could occur if you are expecting to pay off your house in a few years, enter into a reverse mortgage, or downsize. By relocating, you could also significantly change your expenses in retirement. Remember that you cannot predict your retirement expenses with 100 percent certainty, but you can get pretty close by following a process, setting retirement goals, tracking your income and expenses, and reviewing the current economic conditions when you near retirement.

As I discussed earlier, inflation is a huge factor that you need to consider as it removes your purchasing power over time. If you are estimating expenses for your first year of retirement and are still a number of years from retirement, it is appropriate to add an inflation factor to this estimate as well. This topic will be discussed further in Step 5.

Additionally, by categorizing your expenses, you can see where you are spending your money and determine whether any of those items are experiencing higher or lower rates of inflation. For example, health care costs are currently experiencing higher-than-average inflation, while electronics are experiencing deflation.

As you inventory your expenses, some will clearly be essential to your lifestyle, such as mortgage payments, taxes, groceries, and medical insurance premiums. Others may be more discretionary, such as dining out or entertaining. Others yet may even feel like luxuries, such as that trip to Europe—which could be replaced by a less expensive trip to the beach. Making these distinctions may help you begin to identify where you could cut back when necessary. You'll see in Step 9 that you may also want to choose to fund essential expenses with fewer risky approaches than discretionary and luxury expenses.

Rewirement Alert

Many people mistakenly believe that if one spouse dies, expenses will go down. In some cases, expenses can actually go up after the death of one spouse. So, when planning for this contingency, make sure you do not underestimate your expenses.

Action Steps: Estimating Retirement Expenses

Monthly Budget Worksheet

- Housing
    - Mortgage/Rent
    - Real estate taxes
    - Insurance
    - Utilities
    - Other fees and regular maintenance
    - Telephone and cell phone
    - Internet and cable
    - Other
- Food
    - Groceries
    - Dining out
    - Coffee
    - Takeout
    - Other
- Other living expenses
    - Clothing
    - Hair/Beauty
    - Other personal care

- Health care
  - All medical insurance premiums
  - Out-of-pocket costs for health care
  - Out-of-pocket costs for medication and other supplies
- Transportation
  - Car payments
  - Insurance
  - Gas
  - Public transportation

Estimate these other periodic expenses on an annual basis, and divide by twelve for a monthly estimate:

- Education
  - Courses
  - Books and other publications
  - Professional dues
- Taxes
  - Federal
  - State
  - Local
- Entertainment
  - Tickets
  - Transportation
  - Other
- Travel
  - Transportation
  - Hotel
  - Meals
  - Entertainment
  - Gifts
  - Other

- Gifts
  - Christmas or other holiday gifts
  - Birthday gifts
  - Wedding gifts and gifts for other occasions
- Home maintenance and improvements
  - Estimated costs for major home maintenance and repair
  - Estimated costs for home improvements
  - Estimated costs for furniture and other home goods
- Charity
  - Gifts to charity
  - Other expenses

STEP 4—IDENTIFY YOUR SOURCES OF RETIREMENT INCOME

Risk comes from not knowing what you're doing.

—Warren Buffett, Investor

One of the most important questions about retirement income planning is *Where will your income come from once you retire?* Unfortunately, most Americans cannot answer this question. However, the answer is not as difficult as it may seem at first. For instance, most Americans have access to several main assets as they head into retirement. First, there is Social Security, which provides retirement income for the majority of America's retirees. Second, there is home equity, which is often underutilized as a retirement income source. Third, there are the qualified retirement savings from an IRA or an employer-sponsored retirement plan. And lastly, personal savings can play a significant role. These four assets make up the majority of assets available for retirement income. However, they are by no means the only possible sources as some people have business interests, family wealth, and other sources of retirement income to rely on.

When you inventory your sources of retirement income assets, you will need to determine the source of income, how much income it can generate in a year, the impact of inflation on the income source, how long it will generate income, and the reliability of the income source. For instance, Social Security is a federal benefit program run through the Social Security Administration and is funded through payroll taxes. Your benefits are calculated based on the number of years you worked, your income in those years, the age at which you collect benefits, and your full retirement age. As such, you can get a very accurate estimation of your Social Security retirement benefits based on different claiming ages. Additionally, Social Security is protected against inflation as it has cost-of-living adjustments.

Social Security benefits are also payable for life, with a potential survivor benefit for your surviving spouse. However, when you discuss reliability, the answer is not so clear today. Sometime around 2033–2034, Social Security is expected to be able to pay only 77 percent of promised benefits. So, you may want to consider calculating a reduction of benefits into your income source when discussing Social Security. Additionally, Social Security is going to continue to change over the next few years. In 2015, a substantial bit of federal legislation was passed that removed so-called aggressive claiming strategies. Most specifically, the traditional file-and-suspend strategies have all but been eliminated.

If you are asking yourself "How do I know what my Social Security benefits will be?" Social Security does mail out benefit statements every five years. In addition, you can check your projected Social Security benefits online by setting up an online account. It is important to check your benefits each year to make sure that your earnings are correctly tied to your benefits. If you wait too long, you could lose the right to verify and fix your benefits based on your actual earnings. Don't lose those benefits you have worked so hard for; make sure you keep up with your benefit statements. If you are married, consider maximizing the survivor benefit. The survivor is entitled to the higher of his or her own benefit or the survivor benefit. This means you usually want to defer the largest benefit between two spouses until age seventy to maximize the survivor benefit in the event of the first spouse's passing away.

In contrast to Social Security retirement benefits, employer-provided retirement income sources are very different. For example, while a defined benefit plan from your employer will also offer a lifetime benefit that is easily calculated, the benefit will not likely have any cost-of-living adjustments, leaving the benefit subject to a decline in purchasing power over time. While your defined benefit plan likely won't have the level of inflation protection provided by Social Security, these benefits are very secure. In fact, they are prefunded according to federal law and are secured by an insurance program from the Pension Benefit Guaranty Corporation (PBGC).

If you have a 401(k) or other type of defined contribution plan, your benefits will be significantly different than those of a defined benefit plan. While they are both employer-sponsored retirement plans, most defined benefit plans were designed to help you replace a portion of your income in retirement, and most almost always offer payment in the form of a lifetime annuity. If you are married, the required benefit must be offered as a 50 to 100 percent qualified joint and survivor annuity.

A defined benefit plan may also give you the option to elect a lump-sum payment. Choosing the annuity can mean having an excellent base of income that, along with Social Security, can meet your basic income needs for your entire lifetime. It also allows you to be comfortable taking more risk with your other investments. Retirees are often tempted to take the lump sum, and a large percentage do when they are given the option. But be cautious before taking the lump sum—the pension annuity payment is generally larger than what can be purchased outside the plan, and if you decide to invest the lump sum, it means taking the responsibility and risk of choosing investments and determining how much you can withdraw each year.

Rewirement Alert

Too many people take the lump sum option from their employer plan so that they can have access to the money. Instead, think about how it will impact your retirement security; the annuity option could be a much better financial deal.

Defined contribution plans, like your 401(k), are more difficult to manage for retirement income. You essentially have to make your own defined benefit plan. At the time of retirement, your 401(k) plan will likely be distributed to you in the form of a lump sum. While some 401(k) plans offer other forms of payout, they are rarely exercised by the plan participants. This does not mean that taking the lump sum is the correct decision. You should review all the distribution options from your qualified employer plan before making a decision. You should see what the distribution options are and how they fit into your overall retirement income plan. In some cases, the annuities offered in a 401(k) are better than anything you can buy on the open market. Also, if you need more guaranteed retirement income, an annuity distribution option from your 401(k) may be beneficial. In others, the annuity is safer and simpler because you will not need to continue to manage your investment portfolio, and you will not have to take distributions each year to meet your needs. For someone early in retirement, managing investments may seem doable, but will you still want to do that or even have the mental acuity to do that when you are ninety?

In addition to your qualified plan assets, your largest personal financial asset will likely be your home. However, you cannot always list this as a financial asset or a retirement income source. This may bother you at first because you have probably put a lot of money into your home. However, you will always need a place to live in retirement, and this will likely be funded in part by your home equity. Homes are often not good investments but are instead a purchase of housing services. Home values in the United States tend to adjust for inflation but do not otherwise show any other returns. However, this does not mean that buying a home is a bad idea. Owning a home can provide much needed peace of mind and a sense of pride while at the same time reducing housing expenses. Additionally, if used properly, home equity can be an incredibly valuable source of retirement income.

Just remember that as you are moving into retirement, you must start thinking about how you could use your home equity strategically to support your retirement income needs. Are you planning on leaving all the value in your home and passing it as a legacy asset to your children? If so, you may want to ask yourself and your children whether they want the home. Are you going to downsize and sell your home early in retirement, freeing up some of the home equity to spend on other goals? As I discussed earlier, reverse mortgages can be an incredibly valuable tool for generating retirement income. Most importantly, think about your house as an asset. Make your house work for you in retirement. Far too many people leave their home equity untouched throughout retirement and never realize the potential that it holds to generate income and still provide a place to live.

A reverse mortgage, simply put, is a mortgage that does not have to be repaid until you and your spouse permanently leave the home. It can be used a number of ways. Those with conventional mortgages in retirement can reduce their monthly expenses by paying off the existing mortgage with a reverse mortgage. You can also take a line of credit, which can be saved in case there is an emergency or to generate income instead of selling other assets when the market is down. Another option is to receive a stated monthly payment for as long as you remain in the home. A reverse mortgage can also be used in part to purchase a new home in retirement.

Rewirement Alert

Don't just think of your house as a place to live; consider it an income source, a long-term care funding tool, or a legacy asset.

Lastly, make sure you add up all your other individually sourced assets. Make sure you are paying attention to your IRAs, bank account savings, bonds, business interests, collectables, and insurance products. Make sure you are protecting and properly managing all your assets.

As our lives become increasingly digitalized, new risks are developing that challenge traditional asset management and retirement planning techniques. For instance, someone can now steal your money from a bank without ever stepping into the vault. Instances of online fraud and theft are at an all-time high and are expected to continue to rise at a rapid pace. Additionally, as people spend more of their time online and more businesses offer digital services, the management and disposition of digital assets is becoming increasingly complex and important. A decade ago, few business executives were concerned about their digital assets or a digital estate. However, this has changed. Digital assets, if not properly managed, can endanger the strategic plans of their employers, the coworkers who depend on the success of the employer for their own well-being, and their personal beneficiaries. As such, forgetting about valuable online assets can lead to financial loss, lawsuits, complications due to theft or fraud, or a lost source of retirement income.

Digital assets are not your computer and cell phone; they are all the information recorded and stored on those devices. For some people, digital assets are primarily sentimental in value. For example, personal photos, social networks, video games, and e-mail correspondences are worth little monetary value on the open market. However, if you are an executive in a large corporation, running a small business, or blogging online, your digital assets could be worth a tremendous amount of money. This can be a challenging area of the law and business succession planning, so you may want to consider consulting an attorney who can help you maximize your online wealth. This could mean selling a website or transferring ownership of a digital asset. However, all digital assets cannot be transferred, so it's important to take a look at what you are allowed to do. Certain digital assets like Bitcoin and PayPal accounts have clear financial values and should be protected accordingly. You will also need a strategy to convert financial assets like Bitcoin into retirement income.

Cryptocurrencies, like Bitcoin, will continue to grow in popularity and usage. However, as an investment, they are very risky. Putting money into a cryptocurrency is like speculating on increased adoption of that specific crypto. This is hard, if not impossible, to predict with any certainty. So, while I am in favor of having some assets used as a speculative fund, the amount should be small, between 1 and 5 percent of your investment portfolio. The idea is what can you stomach going away completely? If you can't handle losing 5 percent of your wealth, then don't speculate.

You need to have a good understanding of the income sources available to provide you with your retirement income. Once you have accounted for the assets you own, make sure you are protecting them and maximizing the income from each source to meet your needs. As technology, businesses, and economic trends change, your income sources could change also, so pay close attention to your assets—they are the source of your future retirement paychecks!

Action Steps: Identify Potential Retirement Income Sources

- Estimate Social Security benefits based on an expectation of your claiming age.
- Estimate your home's market value, reduced by the outstanding mortgage, to determine available home equity.
- Inventory all employer-provided projected monthly retirement benefits from current or prior employer-provided defined benefit plans.
- Calculate the current account balances in any defined contribution plans as well as current contributions that you and your employer are making to allow a projection of benefits at retirement.
- Add up values of all IRA and Roth IRA accounts, and estimate future contributions in order to allow a projection of benefits at retirement.
- Inventory the current value of any deferred nonqualified annuities (outside your IRA or other tax-advantaged retirement plans), and identify estimates of future premium payments.
- Inventory any projected income payments from any deferred income annuities that you own.
- Add up all other personal savings that you are likely to use to fund your retirement needs. This can include investment accounts, savings and checking accounts, and values of any emergency funds. Again, estimate any additional savings that you expect in order to project the value of these accounts at retirement.
- Identify and estimate the value of any direct business interests (including real estate investments) that you have—you may be anticipating

ongoing income from these interests or proceeds from the sale of these business interests.

- Executives may have additional benefits that they are entitled to from deferred compensation plans or equity-based programs.
- Identify the value of any collections or other personal property that you are expecting to sell to support your retirement needs.
- Look at any cash value life insurance policies that you have and determine the value of any death benefits as well as the cash value of the products.
- Low-income individuals may be eligible for Supplemental Security Income (SSI) in addition to Social Security benefits.
- Review any long-term care insurance policies to identify the available pool of supplemental income that will be available when long-term care is needed.
- Counting on future inheritances as a retirement resource is generally not a good practice unless there is a high degree of certainty that the inheritance will be received.
- Identify whether there are digital assets that will be sold to support retirement needs.
- Values in any health savings accounts (HSAs) can be withdrawn tax-free to pay medical expenses now or in retirement.
- Part-time work can be an important source of income in retirement. Be realistic about the possibility of working and about how much you will earn—statistically, the percentage of pre-retirees who report that they will work in retirement is much higher than the actual percentage of retirees who work.
- Individuals in sales positions may be entitled to residual sales commissions for a short or long period of time after they stop working.

STEP 5—CALCULATE FINANCIAL PREPAREDNESS

Cessation of work is not accompanied by cessation of expenses.

—CATO, PHILOSOPHER

People often ask me about the amount of savings needed to be ready for retirement. Unfortunately, as I discussed before, there is no magic retirement savings number. So, while having $1 million or $2 million or even ten times your salary saved is nice, it's not something that guarantees a secure retirement. While these figures can be helpful as a general guideline, they fall short in determining whether someone is really financially prepared for retirement. Your retirement income security depends in part on how much you save, but it also depends on many other factors, some of which you can control and some of which you cannot. For instance, you will have some control over when you retire, but you will have no control over the inflation rates you experience during retirement. In order to figure out whether you are financially prepared for retirement, you must calculate the amount of income you will be able to generate in retirement.

In order to calculate your potential retirement income, you will need to make several assumptions. Furthermore, to get an accurate calculation, you will likely need to utilize a retirement income software program or calculator. The good news is that there are a lot of user-friendly and free online calculators. Most financial institutions, banks, and investment companies now offer some type of online retirement income calculator. For instance, Vanguard, BlackRock, New York Life, and MarketWatch all offer free retirement income tools. Now, these free tools vary in their level of sophistication and will often use different assumptions in their calculations. This means your projected retirement income may vary from one calculator to another. If you are looking for a more sophisticated retirement income program, there are a variety of programs out there, like Income Discovery, MoneyGuidePro, or Moneytree. Just remember that when using any software program the output is just a projection and is only as good as the assumptions and numbers you put into the software. (Garbage in—garbage out!)

So what are the assumptions and factors you need to consider? Many software applications will have built-in assumptions for a variety of variables. However, it is likely you will have to modify some of them in order to tailor the calculation to your unique situation. First, you need to put in an accurate account of all the resources that could provide you with retirement income. This makes the work you did earlier in your planning even more important! Without an accurate list of potential income sources, there will be no way for you to calculate your projected retirement income. So remember to include your Social Security, 401(k), IRA, annuities, home equity, personal savings, and business interests as well as any other potential sources of retirement income.

Next, you will need to decide on a projected retirement date. This is a very important decision, and while you will not have full control over the exact day you retire, you will likely have some control over when you retire. Some people are forced into early retirement due to declining health, corporate downsizing, or family responsibilities. However, most people are able to retire on their own terms. When you retire is an important decision with regard to your retirement income security. Just working a year or two longer can make all the difference in the world. In fact, working a year or two longer will have a much bigger impact on your retirement income security than saving an additional 5 percent of your salary for the last five years of your employment. When it really comes down to it, the question of when you should retire is the single most important retirement decision you will make.

About 45 percent of people retire earlier than they expected to, about 45 percent of people retire when they expected to, and about 10 percent of people retire later than they expected to live. This means it is just as likely you will retire earlier than you expected to as it is that you will retire when you expected to. With that in mind, you need a contingency plan for an earlier-than-expected retirement date. Run the software calculations based on when you plan to retire, and then run it a few more times and see what happens to your retirement income security if you have to retire two or three years earlier than planned.

Rewirement Alert

Far too many people become complacent and get forced into an unexpected early retirement; plan for the possibility of an early retirement.

Figuring out when you are going to retire helps you set the starting point of your retirement period. However, you will also need to figure out how long your retirement is going to last. This is the longevity or life expectancy assumption that I discussed earlier. In a lot of ways, this is a much more challenging matter than when you will retire because you have far less control over your longevity. An uncertain retirement period creates unique challenges for retirement income planning as at some point, you typically will need to liquidate some of your assets to help meet your expenses. However, the rate at which you can liquidate those assets depends heavily on how long they need to last. By vastly underestimating or overestimating your life expectancy, you may not be able to meet your retirement goals. For instance, if you underestimate your life expectancy, you will likely deplete all your savings well before you pass away. On the flip side, if you overestimate your life expectancy, you may end up holding onto too many assets and not enjoying increased spending while you are alive.

Determining your life expectancy may not be the most enjoyable activity you undertake when planning for retirement as it brings you face-to-face with your own mortality and presents potentially difficult family situations. Life expectancy tables can be used to help you with your calculations. For retirement planning, it is more appropriate to measure life expectancy from the current age of an individual than from his or her birth date. For instance, a person who is sixty-five has a much longer life expectancy at that age than he or she would have if his or her life expectancy had been estimated at birth. Today, someone at age sixty-five has roughly a 25 percent chance of living to age ninety and a 10 percent chance of living to age ninety-five. Unfortunately, most people tend to underestimate their own life expectancy.

If you are planning for yourself and your spouse, remember that the joint life expectancy of a couple is longer than the individual life expectancy of just one person. You should look at a joint life expectancy table to get an accurate projection. Social Security does provide free life expectancy tables online as well as a free online longevity calculator to help you project your life expectancy. The Society of Actuaries also publishes a life expectancy table online. So you may want to check out how long these tables say you have left! I know— what a fun endeavor. But remember that the tables provide only the average, so they're wrong 50 percent of the time!

Other factors besides just your age and available mortality tables should be considered when determining your projected life expectancy. For instance, you should review the life spans of your parents and grandparents. This can give you a general understanding of longevity in your family. Additionally, you should look at your health. If you have a history of major health issues, you may be inclined to lower your life expectancy and increase your expected retirement health care expenses. Those in good health who are living a healthy lifestyle may want to raise that life expectancy number. Also, take into consideration your socioeconomic standing. People in higher socioeconomic groups tend to have longer life expectancies, in part due to better health care systems and better access to preventative care. So, in the end, you want to use the available statistical life expectancy information to first get a starting point and then adjust your life expectancy up or down based on personal factors like family history, health, lifestyle, and socioeconomic status.

The next factor is determining how much income you will need in retirement. We tackled the issue of estimating the first year's income need in Step 3, but in a retirement calculation, expenses must be projected throughout retirement. Part of this exercise requires an expectation about inflation. Inflation is really a measure of how the increase in the cost of living will erode your purchasing power over time. The concept is simple: a dollar today is worth more than a dollar tomorrow.

Since 2000, inflation has remained very low in the United States. However, when choosing an inflation assumption for your calculation, you should pick a long-term inflation number as opposed to the current year's inflation rate or even the average inflation rate of the past ten years. Historically, inflation in the United States has averaged around 3.25 percent. However, in the United States, we have seen thirty-year periods when inflation was 5 percent on average. During other periods, the inflation rate averaged just 2 percent. Risk-averse individuals may want to assume a higher rate of inflation, somewhere in the 3.5 percent to 5 percent range, when calculating their retirement expenses. However, others may feel more comfortable with a lower rate.

There are other factors to consider. For instance, inflation is not consistent across the country. Regional inflation rates can differ drastically from the national rate. Furthermore, you need to consider your own specific spending habits and the spending habits you expect to have in retirement. For a number of years, retirees have experienced higher-than-average inflation on their goods and services. The main reason for this is that health care and long-term care costs have been rising faster than the average inflation rates. Because retirees spend more of their money on health and long-term care services, they are experiencing higher-than-average inflation rates. A more sophisticated software tool will allow for modeling different inflation rates for different expenses.

One countervailing consideration here is that some data shows that retirees do not tend to increase their spending during retirement to keep up with inflation. This is part of what has been seen as a spending pattern in retirement for many that decreases as retirement progresses. The pattern can change later in retirement as costs may increase as additional care is needed. Having at least some changes in spending over retirement makes perfect sense as life can change significantly as retirees age. Again, software programs often allow adjustments in spending over time. These predictions are difficult, but there are a couple adjustments that may be appropriate when planning to address this issue:

- Choose a slightly lower inflation rate to reflect a reduction in spending in retirement.
- Choose a 20 percent reduction in spending after a certain age or after the death of a spouse, with the expectation of life becoming more sedentary.
- Choose an increase in spending later in retirement to reflect the need to pay for additional care—another option is to disregard the additional spending if long-term care insurance is likely to cover the additional expenses.

Even when calculating our retirement income needs, we cannot escape Benjamin Franklin's infamous words asserting that the only certain things in this world are death and taxes. As we have already addressed death in the form of life expectancy, we must now address taxes. When generating retirement income, it is likely that at least a portion of your retirement income will be taxable. For example, distributions from IRAs, 401(k)s, and defined benefit plans are normally tax-deferred savings and will be taxable upon distribution. Other income sources, like annuity payments, will likely be partially taxable and partially a return of your cost basis (what you paid into the annuity). As much as 85 percent of your Social Security benefits are potentially taxable. So, to accurately determine how much income you will have after taxes, you need to make another assumption: your projected retirement tax rate.

It is prudent for me to also mention that tax laws change. In fact, at the end of 2017, we saw one of the largest tax code changes and corporate tax cuts in US history passed into law. However, many of the changes will go away in 2025. So, for a few years, there will be a lot of tax law uncertainty. Unfortunately, you must play the game by the rules that are in place. So, today, you have to deal with the tax laws that exist. I guess the good news is that at least the CPAs and tax attorneys are happy!

Your projected retirement tax rate assumption is a very difficult number to pin down because tax rates evolve drastically over time. As I said before, retirement income planning is like hitting a moving target in the wind. Tax laws, like the wind, can change at a moment's notice. When determining your potential tax rate, you need to consider both federal taxes and state taxes. Certain states do not tax military retirement benefits, for instance, nor do they tax tax-qualified retirement plan distributions like your 401(k). However, other states tax both distributions. Property taxes and state deductions can also vary dramatically. So, if you are planning on relocating in retirement, you will need to examine the local tax rules to see how they will impact your retirement income. Unfortunately, even the most complex software will be able to provide only a rough estimate of your future taxes. Taxes change every single year and will continue to change. You will need to stay on top of new tax laws so that you can understand the impact that they will have on your plan.

There are strategies you can use to reduce your potential tax liabilities. For instance, using life insurance as a retirement income source and taking withdrawals from the cash value will not result in taxable income in most instances. Additionally, properly using a Roth IRA can help you lock in taxes today, hopefully at a lower rate, and reduce your taxable income in retirement. Other planning tools like health savings accounts (HSAs) and long-term care insurance can provide funding for your medical and long-term care costs without resulting in taxable income as qualified distributions from both the HSA and long-term care insurance are income tax–free. Lastly, a reverse mortgage is a loan and is not considered taxable income. As such, if you are concerned about future tax rates and hold the belief that the United States will be in a rising-tax-rate environment for the foreseeable future, you can take advantage of a variety of planning tools to reduce this risk of changing tax rates.

Diversify your investments among accounts with different tax attributes. For example, use a mix of Roth accounts and tax-deferred accounts, like IRAs or 401(k)s, and put some investments in after-tax accounts, like investment brokerage accounts. Also, to the extent possible, hold bonds and income sources taxed as ordinary income in tax-deferred or Roth accounts.

Rewirement Alert

Don't think all investments and advisors are created equal. Fees range dramatically among different investments and advisors. Remember that you don't get what you pay for in fees! Fees bring down your returns over time. This is not to say that advisors don't add value above their fees—they had better—but you should still shop around, even if it's not fun!

In addition to taxes, high investment fees can reduce your available retirement income. Now, don't mistakenly believe that you need to avoid all investment fees. Fees can provide value, so focus on the value you get for your fees as opposed to focusing solely on the amount of the fees. As such, if you are working with a financial advisor, retirement income professional, or investment manager, make sure you understand how these professionals are compensated and how the fees will impact your future retirement income.

The last assumption you need to consider is your rate of investment returns. The returns you experience on your retirement assets will be crucial to determining how long you can make your retirement income last. Historical investment returns are often used to help predict future investment returns. However, remember that past performance does not guarantee future performance. So, while a similar portfolio of investments might have averaged 8 percent historically, it is not guaranteed that the investments will return 8 percent for you moving forward.

In the past, there was a tendency for people to invest more and more conservatively as they aged. However, this approach should be tempered somewhat in light of new research. The best investment practices have moved away from super bond-heavy and conservative investment strategies for retirees. What we see now is that super conservative investment strategies give up too much return over time and put the retiree at a higher risk of running out of money. Considering this, your investment allocation should remain somewhat steady throughout retirement. Common asset allocations consist of 70 percent in stocks and 30 percent in bonds. Even a conservative investment portfolio may have close to a 50:50 stock-to-bond allocation. However, there are people who like the security and reliability of guaranteed income sources and stay away from the market completely.

Retirement Income Calculation Assumptions to Consider

- Sources of retirement income (financial assets)
- Retirement date
- Life expectancy
- Income need
- Inflation
- Tax rates
- Investment fees
- Investment returns

Remember that your investment allocation should be specifically crafted to satisfy your own level of risk tolerance and your own retirement income objectives. One effective strategy you can use to improve the longevity of your investment portfolio is to reduce your equity allocation investments during the last two years of your employment and during the first two years of retirement. By being a little more conservative during these years, you can avoid the risk of a large market drop close to your retirement date. Remember that bond funds are not the same thing as bonds! Even in a low-interest-rate environment, bonds can play an important role as they provide a guaranteed investment return. A 2 percent return may not sound good when compared to the stock market in the long run, but a 2 percent return seems fantastic when a 2008 occurs and the market drops 30 percent in a year. Ultimately, your investment return assumption will be driven by your specific combination of investments.

Action Steps: Calculate Whether Your Plan Is on Track

- Review the software programs mentioned in this step as well as other programs available to you through work or other means.
- Choose a program, and calculate whether your plan is on track.
- Run the numbers with a range of assumptions about when you will retire, inflation rates in retirement, and the return on your investments.
- Consider using at least two different calculators as programs differ in how they calculate the results.
- Recalculate to see whether your plan is on track at least once a year.

STEP 6—DEVELOP A STRATEGY TO ADDRESS ANY SHORTFALL

The root of all evil isn't money; rather, it's not having enough money.

—GENE SIMMONS, MUSICIAN

Once you run the software and compare your potential income to your expected retirement expenses, you will know whether you are financially prepared for retirement. Many software programs may give you a percentage for success, meaning you have enough money to meet your needs based on your assumptions and historical data. You may find out that you have a retirement income shortfall 100 percent of the time or only 5 percent of the time. In either case, it is possible that you do not have enough income sources to meet all your retirement goals and expenses. Now, the real question is if you have a retirement income shortfall, are there any options available for you to address the shortfall and still meet your retirement goals?

There are a variety of strategies to help address a retirement income shortfall. If you have enough time before you are planning on retiring, you could save more money for retirement. However, as you near retirement, this strategy will be less and less effective. Saving money for retirement at an early age will have a much bigger impact than saving money in the few years just prior to retirement. You can also be more efficient with your savings. This means taking advantage of the tax benefits offered by the federal government. When saving for retirement, utilize the tax deductibility of salary deferrals in your employer-sponsored plan and in a traditional IRA to get a better bang for your buck. Saving on a tax-deferred basis will generally result in much higher savings in the long run than saving on an after-tax basis. Be smart, and use the tax-advantaged savings options available to you.

Sometimes all your plan needs is a careful rebalancing of your investments. Perhaps you have too many safe investments, like bonds, in your portfolio. By moving to a more heavily stock-weighted asset allocation investment strategy, you can increase your retirement income and your retirement security without having to save any more money. Additionally, you may have the right bond-to-stock ratio, but you could be too heavily invested in one company. Again, a rebalancing of your investment portfolio to a more diversified allocation could do wonders for your retirement income.

Take a look at why you have a retirement income shortfall. It could be because you don't have enough money saved, you are retiring too early, or you are spending too much. Make sure you have not left yourself exposed to a risk that could potentially undermine all your hard work and planning. For instance, your plan may fail because you project a three-year long-term care event near the end of your life. This long-term care event could cost hundreds of thousands of dollars. As such, maybe you will be better off with insurance to help cover the risk that is undermining your plan. This means you may have enough assets to have a secure retirement but that you need to reorganize them a bit and shift some of the risk to an insurance company.

If you have a projected retirement income shortfall, there may be very little you can do to improve your income. In that case, you will need to focus on the expense side of the equation. This may mean rethinking your retirement goals. Perhaps you won't be able to join the country club you want to or take as many international cruises. Perhaps you will need to downsize sooner than you anticipated. There is a lot you can do on the expense side without giving up those things that provide you with happiness and enjoyment in retirement. Reducing expenses can help to make your money last longer and can improve your retirement income security.

Action Steps: Consider How You Can Improve Your Retirement Security

In this and previous steps, we have talked about ways you can improve your retirement security prior to retirement. It's a good time to stop and ask yourself these questions to see what else you can do:

Saving More

- Do you have a savings plan at work? If so, do you contribute enough to receive the full employer-matching contribution? If you contribute enough to receive the match, do you take advantage of the opportunity to either contribute more or contribute to a Roth IRA?
- Are you self-employed? If so, have you established your own retirement plan, which can be a Simplified Employee Pension (SEP) plan or a solo 401(k) plan?
- If you don't have a savings plan at work, do you contribute to a traditional IRA or Roth IRA?
- If you have a high-deductible health insurance plan at work, do you contribute to an HSA account?

Spending Less

- Have you looked into relocating to a place that could reduce retirement costs?
- Have you evaluated your spending to see whether you are spending on items that don't really mean much to you?
- Are you making the most of your money, looking for bargains and good deals?

Working Longer

- Are you maintaining your employment skills and professional network in case you choose to continue to work?
- Are you managing stress by taking sufficient vacations to avoid burnout at work?

- Are you paying attention to maintaining your health so that you can continue to work if you choose to?
- If you are planning to work part time in retirement, have you given any thought to what you may do?

Deferring Social Security

- Have you looked into the impact of deferring Social Security benefits? Have you tried using the Consumer Financial Protection Bureau Social Security claiming tool?
- Have you considered how you would meet your income needs if you retired and decided to defer receiving Social Security benefits?

Improving Investment Performance

- Have you evaluated your investment mix and investment performance recently?
- Have you figured out or talked to a professional about whether your investments are appropriate given your age and retirement objectives?

STEP 7—DEVELOP A TAX-EFFICIENT WITHDRAWAL STRATEGY

No government can exist without taxation. This money must necessarily be levied on the people; and the grand art consists of levying so as not to oppress.

—FREDERICK THE GREAT, GENERAL AND KING

Let's be honest: No one likes paying taxes. But governments need the money to function. However, you need not pay any more taxes than legally required. In this step of the retirement income planning process, you need to focus on developing a tax-efficient withdrawal strategy. Developing a tax-efficient withdrawal strategy can save you thousands of dollars, but it requires understanding a myriad of federal tax laws and the way each one interrelates to your retirement plan. In order to develop an effective tax-efficient withdrawal strategy, you will need to be aware of the applicable federal and state taxes, understand the impact of required minimum distributions, consider the tax benefits of a Roth IRA conversion, and review the impact of your distributions on the taxation of your Social Security benefits.

Developing a tax-efficient withdrawal strategy can be challenging and often will require the help of a CPA and a financial advisor. If you have multiple types of retirement savings vehicles, a 401(k), IRAs, Roth IRAs, and a brokerage account, you will need to develop a strategy for turning these assets into income in a tax-efficient manner. Certain accounts, like deductible IRAs and 401(k)s, are often tax-deferred accounts that allow you to take a deduction for contributions when you fund them and avoid income taxes on investment growth until you take a distribution in the future. Other accounts, like investment brokerage accounts, are taxable accounts funded with after-tax dollars. This means you already paid taxes in part but still owe taxes on investment gains. In some cases, you will owe taxes each and every year, and in other cases, you will owe taxes just when you sell the investment. There are some tax-exempt accounts, like HSAs, with which you will never pay taxes on that money as long as you use it for a qualified health care expenditure. Additionally, you may have a Roth account of some type, whether in a 401(k), 403(b), or Roth IRA. Roth tax treatment is a little bit different. These accounts are funded with after-tax dollars, but the growth, as long as it is a qualified distribution, comes out tax-free. If you have a mix of these accounts, you will likely need to do some tax planning to minimize your taxes and maximize your income.

The primary purpose of a tax-efficient withdrawal strategy is to improve your retirement income by extending the longevity of your retirement assets through decreased taxes and increased investment gains. A good tax-efficient withdrawal strategy will be uniquely developed for each person or couple to meet their needs and will reflect the complexities of their specific retirement accounts. Additionally, a tax-efficient withdrawal strategy needs to be nimble enough to react to changes in current tax law and an individual's tax situation in a given year.

In order to develop a tax-efficient withdrawal strategy, you need to look at your list of potential income sources that you laid out earlier in your plan. Next, you need to look at the amount of income you need each year. After you know how much income you need, take a quick look at your future guesses for tax rates. Now you can make some decisions on a tax-efficient withdrawal strategy and determine which accounts you will withdraw from first. As a general principle, it is best to take withdrawals from taxable accounts first—that is, your brokerage accounts. Withdrawals from tax-deferred accounts should come next, and lastly, use up your tax-free or Roth accounts. However, in any given year, you may decide to take withdrawals from all three types of accounts.

Not surprisingly, the decision of when to take withdrawals and where to take them from is often driven by your federal income tax rates. Distributions from your taxable accounts, Social Security, pensions, 401(k)s, and IRAs are taxed as ordinary income. Other investment income, such as interest, dividends, and capital gains, will also be subject to federal income taxes—some at capital gains rates and others at ordinary income rates. Because of that, you will need to be aware of your current income tax rate and know how large of a distribution you can take as income each year before you are backed into a higher tax bracket. For example, let's say you are married and filing jointly in 2015 and have $74,900 of taxable income. Any dollar you earn over that amount will now be taxed at 15 percent for federal income taxes as opposed to the 10 percent rate you enjoyed before. This additional 5 percent in taxes could be a big deal, especially if you needed the money that particular year.

There is another federal tax you want to be aware of when planning for retirement income: the Net Investment Income Tax. This relatively new tax took effect in 2013. This tax applies an additional 3.8 percent on the lesser of your net investment income, or the amount of modified adjusted gross income (MAGI) you have over a federally established threshold amount. In general, investment income includes things like interest, dividends, capital gains, non-qualified annuity payments, and rental income. The thresholds are $250,000 for married, filing jointly; $145,000 for married, filing separately; $200,000 for single and head of households; and $250,000 for a qualifying widow(er) with a dependent child. These thresholds are not indexed, so they will remain the same for future years unless Congress enacts new legislation, which at the writing of this book has still not occurred. However, the Trump administration were pushing hard to remove this tax in 2017. While 401(k) and IRA distributions are not investment income for purposes of the tax, they could increase your MAGI and therefore subject some portion of your retirement income to this additional tax.

Another big tax issue is the section 72(t) early withdrawal penalty taxes that apply to the taxable portion of distributions from qualified retirement plans. Generally, if you take a withdrawal from an IRA, a 401(k), or another retirement plan prior to age 59.5, you will be subject to an early withdrawal penalty tax of 10 percent. Now, there are a variety of exceptions to this 10 percent penalty tax. For instance, the 10 percent penalty usually applies just to the taxable portion of the account. So, if you have a Roth IRA, you can withdraw your own contributions, tax-free, without having to worry about the 10 percent penalty tax. However, if you also withdraw gains, you may have to pay the tax. For IRAs, there are a variety of exclusions from the tax: (1) age 59.5, (2) death of the owner, (3) total disability of the owner, (4) qualified education expenses, (5) substantially equal periodic payments, (6) $10,000 for first-time home-buying expenses, (7) paying off an IRS levy of the plan, (8) qualifying medical expenses, and (9) Roth conversions. The rules are slightly different for a 401(k) or other qualified employer-sponsored retirement plans as you cannot use the money for home-buying expenses or qualified higher education costs. Additionally, there is an exception for withdrawals from a qualified employer-sponsored retirement plan that lowers the 59.5 age requirement to age fifty-five if you end your employment with the company the same year you reach age fifty-five or later. However, if you roll your employer-provided plan into an IRA, you are back to the age 59.5 rule as opposed to the lower age fifty-five rule. Remember that this 10 percent penalty tax applies to the entire taxable portion of the distribution and is added right on top of your normal tax rate. If you are going to take a distribution from a retirement account before you turn 59.5, you need to be aware of the 10 percent penalty tax and plan accordingly.

If you need money from your retirement accounts before you hit age 59.5, consider using substantially equal periodic payments (SEPP), which requires you to take close to equal distributions from the account for the longer of five years or age 59.5 to avoid the 10 percent early withdrawal penalty tax.

Rewirement Alert

Relocating can be a powerful tax-saving strategy in retirement. Don't forget that some states do not tax IRA, Social Security, or pension income. You could save thousands of dollars a year by moving to a new state.

There are two big issues that must be examined in addition to your federal income tax rates. First, you should understand the impact of required minimum distributions, and second, you need to be aware of the Social Security tax torpedo. Both of these topics highlight the importance of having a tax-efficient withdrawal strategy in place for your retirement income plan.

In the year when you reach age 70.5 and in each year afterward, you are subject to required minimum distributions (RMDs) from your qualified retirement accounts, such as your 401(k) and IRAs. However, you do have the ability to defer the first year's RMD until April 1 of the following year. While there are a few exceptions to the RMD rules, if you are still working and active in your retirement plan, the general idea is that the government wants you to take withdrawals from your tax-deferred accounts and spend down the assets over your lifetime. A failure to meet your RMD results in a 50 percent excise tax on the amount that is not distributed. In order to calculate your RMD for a given year, you take the previous year's account balance of the account that is subject to RMDs and divide that balance by the remaining number of years in your life expectancy. At that point, you will need to withdraw that amount from the account by the end of the year. The distribution will likely be treated as ordinary income and be subject to income taxes. Additionally, a large distribution could force you into a higher tax bracket rate. As such, you need to be aware of the RMD rules and how they will impact your distributions and taxes in the future.

An RMD could increase your tax rate simply by moving you into a higher income tax bracket. Additionally, an RMD could increase the amount of your Social Security benefits that are subject to taxation, thereby costing you thousands of dollars a year in additional taxes. This concept is often referred to as the Social Security tax torpedo. Social Security benefits can be up to 85 percent taxable depending on your annual provisional income. Provisional income is determined by taking your adjusted gross income, adding on your tax-exempt interest for the year, and then adding on half your Social Security benefits for the year. Even a modest RMD from an IRA or 401(k) could increase your provisional income to a level high enough so that 85 percent of your Social Security benefits would be subject to taxation.

Let's look at an example that illustrates the Social Security tax torpedo. Say you are seventy-six, you have a $1 million IRA, and your remaining life expectancy is twenty-two years. This means you take the $1 million and divide it by twenty-two, which is $45,454.54. As a single individual, or as a married couple filing jointly, your Social Security benefits are now 85 percent taxable. Now, the real question is *Was there anything you could have done to avoid the higher taxes?* The answer is yes. That planning opportunity takes place during the development of a tax-efficient withdrawal strategy. If you had at one time, or over the course of a number of years, converted your IRA into a Roth IRA, you could have avoided the RMD. A Roth IRA conversion would have brought the $1 million IRA into your income at the time of the conversion. You would have then had an account that would not be subject to RMDs while you were alive, and the Roth IRA and all qualified distributions would have come out income tax–free, not impacting your provisional income or adjusted gross income. As such, you could have had the same amount of income, avoided the RMD, and reduced the amount of taxes you owe on your Social Security benefits.

A tax-efficient withdrawal strategy can save you thousands of dollars a year in taxes. Look for years in which you have an abnormally low tax rate, perhaps when you retire, and consider converting some money into a Roth IRA. Try to minimize the negative impacts of RMDs by planning ahead and seeing how they will impact other taxes and benefits. Lastly, try to keep your tax-advantaged accounts for as long as possible as they will generate more income over time than your taxable accounts. By paying attention to these key tax issues, you can plan around higher taxes and improve your retirement security.

As I discussed earlier, taxes changed dramatically after the 2017 Tax Cuts and Jobs Act was passed. In 2018, a number of deductions were removed, and tax rates were changed. The tax bill changes highlighted the need to do annual tax planning and also served as a great reminder of public policy risk. However, the tax bill itself left most of retirement planning and retirement laws untouched. Still, the tax brackets did change and are listed below. Additionally, I have listed the provisional income that is needed to subject Social Security benefits to taxation. These ranges were not changed in the recent tax law updates.

Unmarried Individuals Other Than Surviving Spouses and Heads of Households

If taxable income is:	The tax is:
Not over $9,525	10 percent of taxable income.
Over $9,525 but not over $38,700	$952.50, plus 12 percent of the excess over $9,525.
Over $38,700 but not over $82,500	$4,453.50, plus 22 percent of the excess over $38,700.
Over $82,500 but not over $157,500	$14,089.50, plus 24 percent of the excess over $82,500.
Over $157,500 but not over $200,000	$32,089.50, plus 32 percent of the excess over $157,500.
Over $200,000 but not over $500,000	$45,689.50, plus 35 percent of the excess over $200,000.
Over $500,000	$150,689.50, plus 37 percent of the excess over $500,000.

Married Individuals Filing Separate Returns

If taxable income is:	The tax is:
Not over $9,525	10 percent of taxable income.
Over $9,525 but not over $38,700	$952.50, plus 12 percent of the excess over $9,525.
Over $38,700 but not over $82,500	$4,453.50, plus 22 percent of the excess over $38,700.
Over $82,500 but not over $157,500	$14,089.50, plus 24 percent of the excess over $82,500.
Over $157,500 but not over $200,000	$32,089.50, plus 32 percent of the excess over $157,500.
Over $200,000 but not over $300,000	$45,689.50, plus 35 percent of the excess over $200,000.

Portion of Social Security Benefits Subject to Federal Income Taxation

Filing Status	Provisional Income Threshold	Amount of Benefits Subject to Federal Income Taxation
Single	Under $25,000	0%
Single	$25,000 to $33,999	Up to 50%
Single	$34,000 or more	Up to 85%
Married Filing Jointly	Under $32,000	0%
Married Filing Jointly	$32,000 to $43,999	Up to 50%
Married Filing Jointly	$44,000 or more	Up to 85%
Married Filing Separately	$0	Up to 85%

- Is your tax burden lower than normal this year? This can be due to a large charitable deduction or a year of lower-than-normal income, or you may be early in retirement and living on resources that are not heavily taxed. If any of the above applies to your situation, it is a good time to consider converting a portion of your IRA to a Roth IRA.
- Are you close to retirement and at your maximum earnings capacity? In that case, you may want to maximize deductible contributions to reduce your current income. Once in retirement, you may have the opportunity to take withdrawals or convert to a Roth IRA at a lower-than-normal tax rate.
- Do you have almost all your retirement assets in tax-deferred retirement plans? If you have only tax-advantaged savings, all your income will be taxable in retirement. If tax rates go up or you need a large withdrawal for a purpose, you will be stuck paying higher taxes. By developing sources of income with either no tax burden (Roth IRAs) or a lower tax burden (taxable accounts and nonqualified annuities), you will have more flexibility in retirement.
- Can you take some withdrawals from your tax-deferred plan at a lower-than-normal tax rate? If you are in early retirement, you may want to first take withdrawals from taxable investments, but you will also want to take some withdrawals from a tax-deferred plan to take advantage of a lower tax rate.
- If you are in retirement, do you have any big expenses coming up this year? If you take the extra amount out of your IRA, you may end up paying a higher tax rate. You may instead choose to take withdrawals from an account that does not have tax consequences. This could be a Roth IRA, a life insurance policy, or even a reverse mortgage line of credit.

STEP 8—UNDERSTAND THE RISKS FACING YOUR PLAN

The four most dangerous words in investing: "this time it's different."

—SIR JOHN TEMPLETON, INVESTOR

You need to understand the risks that could derail your retirement income plan. There are many risks you could face in retirement and a variety of options available to help you manage these risks. Risks are those uncertain events that could adversely impact your plan. Some of these may be personal in nature, such as chronic health problems or the need for long-term care, while others may be market-wide disruptions such as hyperinflation.

Two different concepts are important to consider when discussing risks: risk tolerance and risk capacity. First, consider your risk tolerance level. This is finding out how comfortable you are with risk. What keeps you up at night? The second issue to consider is your risk capacity. This is your ability, and the ability of your plan, to handle risk. For example, you may be a very risk-tolerant person when it comes to inflation, but your plan may not have any risk capacity and be subject to a lot of inflation risk because your major sources of income do not have any cost-of-living protections against a decline in purchasing power over time. As such, risk tolerance and risk capacity often do not relate to each other. However, let's look at the risks you could encounter and determine what type of impact they would have on your plan.

Risk management techniques are important to understand when dealing with risk. First, you need to understand the risks you face and analyze how they would impact your retirement security. For a lot of risks, you may look at the worst-case scenario and stress test your plan for that worst-case event's occurring. Could you handle, say, a substantial long-term care event or 5 percent average inflation? If your answer is no, then you need to decide how you want to tackle that specific risk factor. There are a variety of options available. First, you may decide to reduce the risk you face. Not all risks can be managed this way, but some can. For example, you can reduce health care risk by living a healthier lifestyle and engaging in preventative care. In some cases, you can also avoid risks. For instance, if you are worried about the uncertainties of investment performance (market risk), you could choose to invest only in low-risk investments—although that is not advised here! You can also transfer risk to someone else. For example, if you are concerned about outliving your money, you could transfer longevity risk to an insurance company by buying an inflation-protected longevity annuity that would make annual payments for the rest of your life. However, the exact strategy you will employ for dealing with risk will depend on your risk tolerance, your risk capacity, and the specific risk. Lastly, in some cases, you may just want to avoid escalating your risk. The risk of financial elder abuse, for instance, is more likely for those individuals who have large liquid savings on hand. As such, you may engage in behavior that would not escalate that risk during retirement. Properly utilizing these risk management strategies can help to protect retirement income security and bring peace of mind to even the most worried retiree.

Action Steps: Prepare for the Risks You Face in Retirement

Below are the most critical retirement risks and some of the key risk management techniques that need to be addressed. This is a complex subject, which I covered in much more detail earlier on in the book.

Longevity Risk

- **Issue**: The uncertainty of how long retirement will last is one of the most challenging aspects of retirement income planning. Living longer means a more expensive retirement as resources need to last longer and other risks—such as health care costs, long-term care costs, and inflation—are all exacerbated by a long life.

- **Solutions**: This risk can be transferred by creating sources of income that pay for as long as you live. Options include deferring Social Security (to get a larger annuity payment), electing an annuity form of distribution from your company-sponsored retirement plan, or buying a commercial annuity that promises lifetime income. Another option is adding sources of income that pay for an indefinite period of time, like rental income from investment property. If you are relying on withdrawals from your portfolio to support your income needs, you need to carefully consider the investment mix and how much you withdraw each year.

Investment Risks

- **Issue**: Individual investments carry a number of risks, and even investing in a diversified portfolio is risky as the market as a whole is quite volatile. Volatility is especially troublesome as you approach retirement as hitting a savings target on a specific date is quite difficult. In addition, when you begin to take withdrawals from a portfolio, whether you have positive or negative returns in the first few years of retirement has an impact on how long a portfolio will last.
- **Solutions**: Even though investment risk creates some uncertainty, research shows that retirees cannot afford *not* to take some market risk—in fact, many studies have shown that a 40 to 50 percent equity exposure in retirement is needed to address the risk of inflation and increases the probability that the portfolio will last a lifetime. One approach to address this challenge in retirement income planning is to choose a bifurcated investment strategy with investments and products with little or no market risk, chosen to meet basic needs, and more market risk, taken to address discretionary and unexpected expenses and legacy goals. Other ways to reduce market risk include the following:

- Having the lowest exposure to equities in the years nearest retirement age—when a bad order of negative returns can have the most negative impact.
- Considering market conditions when choosing how much to withdraw—lowering withdrawals in years of negative performance reduces the risk of failure.
- Reducing the volatility in the portfolio by increasing diversification (i.e., adding more asset classes)—for example, adding small company and international stocks and adding alternative asset classes like real estate and commodities.

Inflation Risk

- **Issue**: When you are working, the impact of inflation is often offset by an increase in your salary. In retirement, inflation reduces the purchasing power of income as goods and services increase in price. This can mean a reduction in your standard of living unless you have the resources to increase your income to keep up with inflation. To see the erosive impact of inflation, try the online Department of Labor inflation calculator[1].
- **Solutions**: A way to address inflation is to build income streams that increase with inflation. The easiest way to do this is by deferring Social Security benefits, as this will lead to a higher percentage of retirement income that is subject to annual cost-of-living increases. Other options include building income streams with Treasury Inflation-Protected Securities (TIPS) and buying certain types of annuities. The other primary option is to invest in asset classes that are likely to do well in inflationary times. Investments in real estate are one such category as unanticipated inflation often correlates with increasing real estate returns. Investing in equities can also provide a limited hedge

---

1 See https://www.bls.gov/data/inflation_calculator.htm.

on inflation. International equities may provide an even better hedge as inflation is often associated with depreciation of home currency.

Medical Expense Risk

- **Issue**: Costs for health care generally become more expensive and unpredictable as we age. Costs increase in retirement in part because the employer is no longer paying for part of the insurance premium. If you retire before age sixty-five, that can mean buying an individual policy or going into the health care exchange. If you retire after age sixty-five, it generally means paying premiums for Medicare Parts B and D and Medicare Supplement policies. Even with insurance, some expenses are not included. For example, Medicare does not cover dental care or hearing aids. Also, chronic or acute illnesses may mean more significant and unexpected out-of-pocket expenses.

- **Solutions**: Planning for unexpected health care costs begins with choosing the appropriate insurance. For those aged sixty-five and older who are eligible for Medicare, there are many critical decisions that must be made. You can choose traditional Medicare Parts A and B, purchase drug coverage under Medicare Part D, and cover the gaps in coverage through a private Medicare Supplement policy. As an alternative, you can choose Medicare Advantage instead, which is a managed care approach that may provide more services at a lower cost in exchange for a limited network of providers. Proper planning also means planning to have sufficient funds to cover noncovered services. Those who retire before age sixty-five are often surprised at just how much it costs to purchase individual coverage. Working to age sixty-five has the benefit of eliminating what can otherwise be a very expensive period to cover with private insurance.

Other Risks Associated with Aging

- **Issues**: As retirees age and begin to have more physical limitations, they may have to hire others to perform duties around the house that they once did themselves. In addition, cognitive limitations can require their choosing family members or professionals to help them make financial decisions. Frailty can also increase the possibility of elder financial abuse. At some point, chronic diseases, orthopedic problems, and Alzheimer's can prevent a person from living alone, which will require financial resources for custodial and medical care.
- **Solutions**: The aging process brings on many challenges that require planning. Planning begins with recognizing these contingencies and talking to your family members about how you want to be cared for. Planning also includes drafting powers of attorney and trusts that allow for the transfer of control over decision making to those you most trust. Planning also requires considering how to pay for long-term care if the need arises. This means considering whether there are family members willing to provide care, the feasibility of purchasing long-term care insurance, the option of using a reverse mortgage to fund long-term care costs, and whether government programs are available to pay for services.

Public Policy Risk

- **Issue**: As I have said many times now, planning for retirement is like hitting a moving target in the wind. Your target moves because your life expectancy and goals will continue to change throughout retirement. The wind is similar to public policy risk. Taxes, laws, public policy, and government programs will change while you are planning for retirement and when you are retired. You may have been planning on having certain benefits from Medicare, Medicaid, or Social Security, but the government often improves, reduces, and tinkers with the programs, removing key benefits and adding others over time. These changes to Medicare, Medicaid, Social Security, and tax law can have significant impacts on your retirement income plan.

For example, significant changes to Social Security occurred late in 2015 with the passage of the Bipartisan Budget Act of 2015. These changes are the most significant changes to Social Security that have been seen in the past decade. The goal of these changes was to remove certain "aggressive" claiming strategies and improve the overall funding status of Social Security. However, in the process, certain Americans—some nearing retirement—lost a great deal of potential future Social Security income. In some cases, couples lost over $50,000 due to the Social Security changes. The lost benefits upset many people who felt that the rug had been pulled out from under them just a few years before retirement. This is important for everyone moving forward because Social Security is facing funding issues and could run out of money somewhere around 2033–2034 if nothing changes. However, government accounting is not like accounting for normal people. As such, Social Security does not really run out of money, nor does it have giant trust funds today. Instead, it is all a bit fictional. However, at some point, the system will be changed, whether in the way of reduced benefits, increased taxes, or a mix of both. But expect Social Security to remain in some shape or form as far too many Americans rely on the system for us to just cut it out completely. The country would collapse, and I don't think anyone in Washington, DC—Republican or Democrat—is looking for that to happen.

So what happened with Social Security? Two major changes occurred: (1) the extension of the deemed filing rule from full retirement age to age seventy and (2) the removal of most file-and-suspend strategies. The extension of the deemed filing rule applies to everyone who was not age sixty-two by the end of 2015. Sorry, millennials, this strategy is not around for you. The reality is that it's not around for many people at all anymore. Before the rule change, if you were eligible for a worker's benefit and a spousal benefit at the same time and you claimed benefits prior to full retirement age, the deemed filing rule applied, and you would simply receive the larger of the two benefits. However, if you waited until full retirement age to claim, you could choose the spousal benefit at full retirement age and defer your worker's benefit, allowing it to continue to grow until you turned seventy. In this way, you could receive some income immediately and still take advantage of receiving the deferred worker's benefit at age seventy. This has been changed; now, anyone filing for benefits will receive the larger of either the worker's benefit or the spousal benefit, as you are deemed to have filed for the larger of the two benefits at any time you file.

In conjunction with the extension of the deemed filing rule, the new laws removed the ability to voluntarily file and suspend your Social Security benefits for the purposes of either (1) triggering a spousal benefit for a spouse or (2) protecting the right to file for retroactive benefits. The ability to take advantage of this file-and-suspend strategy ended back in 2016. However, something like this could come around again. So pay careful attention to the changes that will occur to Social Security. The reality is that the system will continue to change, which could bring forth new claiming or planning opportunities.

The Social Security changes are worth talking about in their own right, but let's highlight the impact of public policy risk with a current and relevant example.

- **Solutions**: Public policy risk is one of the most difficult risks to plan for because we cannot control when or how the government decides to change the laws. However, one way to minimize the risk and impact of public policy changes is to diversify your retirement income and diversify your savings accounts among a variety of asset classes and accounts. For instance, if your only retirement income is Social Security, any reductions to Social Security will hit you hard. However, if you can add in other sources of income, you can minimize the impact of legal changes to the current system. The same is true for any government program. The more dependent you are on one or two government laws or programs, the more public policy risk you face. Potential future public policy changes are not as impactful if you have a variety of asset classes, diversify the taxation of your savings (Roth, tax-deferred, and after-tax accounts), and build in some financial flexibility to account for any reduction in Medicare or Social Security in the future.

Timing Risk

- **Issue**: Timing risk refers to the variations in sequences of actual events that can have a significant impact on retirement security. Depending on when you retire, you have to face certain conditions. For example, today's retirees face historically low returns on bonds, CDs, and other fixed-income investments.
- **Solutions**: Planning for these circumstances that are outside your control is more about staying knowledgeable and nimble and taking the appropriate steps to address current market, inflation, tax, and other considerations that affect retirement security. For example, when fixed-income investment returns dropped a number of years ago, some retirees continued investing in CDs and just accepted lower returns instead of considering a different, more appropriate investment strategy. One of the many reasons to work with a skilled financial advisor who is knowledgeable about retirement income planning is that he or she can help you address whatever the challenges of the day may be.

STEP 9—CONVERT ASSETS INTO INCOME

I advise you to go on living solely to enrage those who are paying your annuities. It is the only pleasure I have left.

—Voltaire, philosopher

In the past, retirement income planning was relatively simple for many as it was common for retirees to have enough monthly income from Social Security and company pensions to meet most retirement expenses. When that is the case, personal savings could be used primarily to meet extra and extraordinary expenses. Today, the more common scenario is that retirees have two main retirement resources: Social Security benefits and a savings account—often accumulated in the company's 401(k) plan. In this case, generating retirement income means converting the 401(k) or other assets into an income stream. Another complication is that in today's investment environment, earnings from fixed-income investments (such as bonds and CDs) are quite low, making it difficult to generate sufficient income from investments. While most people would like to be able to live off the income that is generated from their savings, strategies today generally require individuals to invest for total returns with the expectation that they will have to sell some investments over the course of retirement to fund their income needs.

So retirement income planning requires almost everyone—apart from those lucky few who still have defined benefit pension plans—to make hard decisions about how they will generate income from their assets. There are a number of approaches. One option is to simply take regular withdrawals from a diversified portfolio. Withdrawals can consist of income, dividends, and proceeds from the sale of assets. Another option is to buy an annuity that pays a promised benefit for life. A third option is to buy a portfolio of individual bonds that will be liquidated over a specific period of time—with this approach, income is created from a combination of principal and interest payments. An alternative to this third approach is to buy a term certain annuity that promises a specific income payment for a set number of years.

When you are deciding which approach to use, it is helpful to consider how academics and practitioners look at this issue. Many academics use a framework called life cycle investment theory. Under this theory, retirement goals are prioritized. For most retirees, meeting basic or essential expenses in retirement is the highest priority, followed by meeting discretionary income goals and leaving a legacy for their heirs. With this framework, it makes sense to choose assets with little risk when funding the most important goals. This means using bonds, CDs, TIPS, or annuities to build an income floor that at least meets basic expenses. Other goals can be funded with riskier assets, and income needs can be taken from portfolio withdrawals.

In contrast, there are practitioners who don't see much benefit in using annuities and other low-risk investments to build an income floor. They argue that as long as the retiree limits withdrawals to a safe withdrawal rate, staying fully invested provides for more potential for growing assets, which can be used to increase spending or build a legacy. The primary limitation of this approach is the lack of guarantee.

Even those who choose the life cycle flooring approach to planning will want to maintain some of their assets in a portfolio. There are two primary approaches to managing the portfolio part of the plan. The first is managing a single portfolio invested for total returns and taking systematic withdrawals. Annual distributions can be taken from interest, dividends, or the sale of assets. The plan should identify a specified withdrawal rate. If the goal is to get a fixed distribution that keeps up with inflation, the withdrawal amount can be based on the initial value of the portfolio with increases each year for inflation.

The second approach is the bucket approach, in which the portfolio is divided into multiple portfolios, each one meant to meet a specific retirement need. One option creates three to five portfolios to meet income needs for different periods in retirement. You may have a portfolio to provide income for the next five to ten years of retirement, another for the following ten years, and a third portfolio to provide you with income for your remaining ten years of retirement. With this option, the near-term bucket will have the most conservative investments as more certainty is needed to meet the near-term need. As such, bonds and other secure income sources, like annuities, are used to help fund your first few years of retirement. The second bucket may have a mix of bonds and stocks, and finally, the long-term bucket may include riskier assets. Utilizing the bucket approach can be helpful as it allows you to see the purpose of each of the portfolios you have and recognize each one's place and value in your overall plan. It can also help you leave stocks alone so that they can continue to grow in the long-term bucket because you have secure income sources in the near term. You can thereby avoid reactionary stock selling in bad markets since you know that the stocks are for a distant time and not for your income today!

If you choose to take systematic withdrawals from your portfolio or use the bucket approach, a key question will be how much you can afford to withdraw each year. There has been a lot of research on this question, starting with financial expert William Bengen's research project in the 1990s. His research determined that with a 50:50 stock-to-bond portfolio, you could withdraw 4 percent of the initial portfolio value with adjustments for inflation each year and not run out of money during any thirty-year period in the United States since the 1920s. This 4 percent figure is referred to as the safe withdrawal rate and is considered a reasonable rule of thumb on how much you can afford to withdraw. For example, if you had $1 million today, under the safe withdrawal rule, you could take out $40,000 a year for retirement, adjusted for inflation each year, and expect that your resources could support this withdrawal for at least thirty years. It is important to understand that there is no certainty that your money will last this long, as the future may not look like the past. There are a number of studies questioning whether the 4 percent rule is still safe today, given the low returns on fixed-income investments.

What is most important to understand is that when you choose to take distributions from your portfolio, you are essentially self-insuring for the risks that could undermine your plan. It requires that you are very conservative in how much you withdraw to meet all possible market conditions.

When choosing how much you can withdraw, the 4 percent rule of thumb is a good place to start. If you are more conservative, you may choose to lower the amount somewhat. You can also make adjustments based on a number of factors:

- If your retirement period is shorter than thirty years, you can increase the safe withdrawal rate.
- If you increase diversification by adding small-cap and international stocks, you can increase the withdrawal rate somewhat.
- If you are willing to take the risk that you will have to reduce your spending later, you can increase the withdrawal rate. For many, this is a reasonable trade-off, as they may want to travel more or do other things early in retirement and expect to be less active later in retirement.
- If you are willing to reduce your withdrawals when the portfolio has negative returns, you can sustain a slightly higher withdrawal rate.

Action Steps: What's the Best Retirement Income Strategy for You?

- What are your retirement income priorities? The best strategy is the one that best suits your goals. You should start off by asking yourself what is more important: making sure that your income does not go below a certain level, the possibility that you could spend more, or leaving a legacy for your family. When your most important concern is meeting basic expenses, solutions that involve building an income floor make the most sense. If you are more concerned about the possibility of increasing spending or leaving a legacy, then strategies that primarily involve taking withdrawals from your investments may be more appropriate.

- How well funded are you for retirement? If you have more resources than you need to meet your income goals, you have more choices. In this case, some choose to take more risks because they can while others choose to take fewer risks because they don't need to. Unfortunately, many are more marginally funded for retirement, and in that case, the choice in strategy really matters. Maybe the most important advice in this case is to defer Social Security benefits as long as possible and work to reduce spending. Arguably, retirees with limited resources benefit from a balanced approach, building an income floor with annuity income so that they feel more comfortable taking more risks on the investment side.

- How much complexity can you handle? The approach that you choose needs to be one that you can manage. If you are working with a skilled advisor, the plan can be more complex—but even then, complexity is a consideration. A plan that includes income annuities and equity-based mutual funds is relatively simple and quite sound.

- How much lifetime income do you already have? There are still many retirees who earn monthly income from employer-sponsored retirement plans. When this is the case, monthly income may meet most or all their income needs in combination with Social Security benefits. In this case, other assets should stay invested to meet contingent needs. A case can be made for investing these assets more aggressively as the monthly income is comparable to investing in bonds.

STEP 10—RETIRE, AND PUT THE PLAN IN MOTION

I love it when a plan comes together.

—COLONEL JOHN "HANNIBAL" SMITH, *THE A-TEAM*

The last part of the plan is to retire and put the plan in motion. It is likely that you will need the assistance of an insurance professional, a financial planner who specializes in retirement planning, an attorney, a CPA, and an investment advisor at some point to enact a comprehensive plan. Be sure to look at their credentials to make sure that they are all suitable and legitimate professionals. For financial planners, look for well-recognized designations that indicate a comprehensive knowledge level, like the CFP, ChFC, CLU, or CFA designation. Furthermore, you will want to consider finding a financial planner who is a retirement income specialist holding the well-established Retirement Income Certified Professional (RICP) mark. Also, ask around. Word of mouth is a great way to find a good advisor.

While using an advisor will cost money, it is well worth the expense. However, only 52 percent of pre-retirees and 44 percent of retirees consult an advisor according to a Society of Actuaries report, *Understanding and Managing the Risks of Retirement*, which discusses the findings of their Retirement Risk Survey. The report highlights a variety of concerns faced by both pre- and post-retirees, including concerns about health care, long-term care, inflation, and running out of money in retirement. With roughly 96 percent of pre-retirees and 89 percent of retirees responding that they were concerned, to some degree, about their long-term financial future in retirement, it is troubling that only about 50 percent of people meet with a financial advisor. Gaining confidence and peace of mind is just one of the more obvious reasons to seek the services of a financial advisor. Most people in the baby boomer generation are not confident that they will have enough money for retirement. According to research, baby boomers with financial advisors are twice as likely to feel confident about their retirement savings as those without an advisor.

Adding to one's confidence in his or her retirement plan is not the only thing that advisors do. In fact, retirement advisors are well equipped to help America reduce its retirement income shortfall of nearly $4.3 trillion. An international HSBC study, the Future of Retirement, showed that those with financial plans accumulated nearly 250 percent more retirement savings than those without a financial plan in place. Furthermore, nearly 44 percent of those who have a financial plan in place save more money each year for retirement.

Research attempts have been made to quantify into real numbers the value that financial planners can provide. A Morningstar research paper shows that making good retirement income decisions can help individuals generate roughly 1.82 percent excess return each year, creating roughly 29 percent higher retirement income wealth. This means that even if an advisor is charging a 1 percent annual fee for the management of retirement assets, the financial advice provided still has a huge impact on the generation of additional retirement income.

Even if you have a retirement income plan in place, a retirement advisor can still add value. For instance, retirement advisors offer a tremendous amount of value by dealing with extremely complex tax issues, investment choices, and emotional decisions that impact one's financial well-being. Furthermore, they make their clients more secure for retirement, increase their clients' wealth, and help them feel more confident about their financial status. However, not all advisors are created equal, and a few tips should be followed when looking for a retirement planner.

First, retirement advisors are not just for the wealthy, but they do cost money. In fact, due to evolutions in the compensation models, there are advisors available for almost everyone. There are planners out there who focus exclusively on high wealth, middle wealth, or low wealth individuals. However, it is still very important to pay attention to how your retirement advisor is compensated, as fees and compensation matter. If you are worried about how much a retirement planner costs, there are still other options. Many employers offer seminars and some basic financial planning presentations—led by financial advisors—that can provide valuable information and education to their employees.

Second, make sure you have the right retirement advisor for your unique situation. While there are many qualified advisors out there, some may be better trained, better educated, and more suited for your particular needs. Some advisors focus on wealth accumulation while others focus on retirement income planning. Additionally, some advisors specialize in working with same-sex clients, clients with special needs children, or veterans. In order to find an advisor who suits your needs, use a tool like DesignationCheck.com, which can help you locate a certified advisor in your area. For instance, you can search for professional advisors based on your area, or you can even search for advisors with a specific designation that focuses on retirement or health care.

Lastly, do your homework on specific retirement planners before you agree to work with anyone. The CFP Board provides a way to verify CFP certifications and allows consumers to see any disciplinary action taken against a CFP certification holder.[2] Asking your friends, work colleagues, and family members can also be one way to find a financial planner. Also, do not be afraid to ask your financial planner for a client recommendation or testimonial. Financial advisors can add a lot of value for their clients, and if America is going to reduce the retirement income shortfall for baby boomers, financial advisors will definitely be part of the solution for many years to come.

You or your advisor will also have to coordinate all these different decisions and the members of your retirement income team. If you want long-term care insurance, an annuity, stocks, mutual funds, and a risk assessment, you will need help. As such, you may find yourself with a whole army of advisors handling different aspects of your life, your finances, and your future. But are your attorneys, accountants, financial planners, investment brokers, money managers, insurance agents, and retirement advisors all on the same page when it comes to planning for your retirement? In many cases, the answer is simply no. That is, your many different advisors typically do not take the initiative to

2 See https://www.cfp.net/about-cfp-board/ethics-enforcement/disciplined-individuals-by-state

coordinate their efforts and often do not have all the information they need to effectively develop an integrated, holistic retirement plan for you.

Someone will have to manage this team to help them—and you—build a coherent and cohesive retirement income plan. Do not let the fact that you may have to work with multiple people scare you away from getting help. In fact, each type of professional is often an expert in a specific area that needs specialized attention. However, it is crucial that you or your representative perform the following tasks to better ensure the assembly of a successful retirement advisor team:

- **Pick the Right Advisors**: Assembling a successful team of advisors starts with choosing the right people. First, you should check the advisors' credentials and make sure they are all up-to-date with their designations, professional service groups, and other professional requirements—and ask for references. The client should have a very clear understanding of any given advisor's specialty area, what services the advisor will be providing, and how the client will be charged for these services.

- **Have the Right Number of Advisors**: All your advisors should serve a specific purpose by providing you with valuable advice and services. When planning for retirement, you may want to consider having an insurance agent, an investment professional, an attorney, an accountant, and a financial professional to coordinate your retirement plan. However, a client should not be too hesitant to replace an advisor who is not performing. Additionally, while relationships are important, employing family members or close personal friends can become unpleasant if the business relationship turns sour.

- **Identify a Coach**: Your financial advisor will often be the coach of your advisor team. This person will help you implement your retirement plan, assist you in developing a strong team of advisors, monitor your plan, and set forth a strategy to update your plan in case of unforeseen problems or changes. Without a good coach, your retirement advisor team could be left without the proper direction and guidance to successfully develop, monitor, implement, and coordinate a unified retirement plan tailored to meet your goals and needs.

- **Prioritize Your Goals**: In order for your advisors to be effective in meeting your retirement objectives, you need to know what you want in retirement. One great way to prioritize goals is to test-drive retirement by phasing into it slowly instead of retiring all at once. By previewing retirement, you can start to do some of the things you want to do in retirement, enabling you to fine-tune your plan to meet your priorities. Previewing retirement also gives you an opportunity to select the activities and goals that will be most important to you in retirement.

- **Verbalize Your Goals**: After you determine and prioritize your retirement goals, you need to communicate these goals to your advisors. This also means keeping your advisors up-to-date on your priorities, as your goals will likely evolve as you enter different stages of your life. Your advisor team cannot help you meet your goals if they are not clearly defined and communicated.

- **Inform Your Advisors of One Another**: Your advisors need to know you are working with other advisors. If you do not make sure your estate attorney knows you are also working with a retirement advisor, you could undermine certain aspects of his or her work on your retirement plan. It is not a bad idea to gather some or all your advisors together at a meeting to ensure that they all know their unique roles in your retirement planning process. This could be difficult to coordinate, but it could also be extremely valuable.

5

Concluding Thoughts

"Jumping to conclusions is efficient if the conclusions are likely to be correct and the costs of an occasional mistake acceptable."

—DANIEL KAHNEMAN, NOBEL PRIZE WINNING BEHAVIORAL ECONOMIST AND PSYCHOLOGIST

I figured it was fitting to close with a quote from Nobel Prize winning behavioral economist Dr. Daniel Kahneman. Retirement is not a place to jump to conclusions about how finances and planning works. The whole notion of *Rewirement* is all about changing the way you think about planning for retirement. It is about breaking down misconceptions, taking affirmative planning steps, and overcoming behavioral biases. However, in many cases, you can't do it alone. And that is perfectly normal, perhaps even rational behavior. Planning for retirement is extremely difficult and can feel daunting at times. There are so many considerations that can make it seem overwhelming. Use the help that is available: an entire industry and several professions developed to help you with this journey. A comprehensive retirement advisor can add a lot of value to your plan and help you make good financial decisions that will improve your retirement. An advisor can also help you maximize your income sources and make adjustments over time. Retirement planning is not a one-time event but a continuous process that needs to adjust to changes in your life, the market, and legal standards.

Retirement is not all about finances, but good financial decisions allow you to pursue the many activities that will make your retirement enjoyable. Making good retirement income decisions for yourself can also help your spouse, your children, and your friends, enabling you to live a financially independent life without becoming a financial burden. Running out of money in retirement is a real risk, even for wealthy individuals who do not plan for their future. While failing to plan does not guarantee you will run out of money, it does increase the odds that you will not be able to meet your retirement goals. Don't throw away decades of hard work by making ill-informed decisions that could cost you your financial security in retirement.

If there is one thing to take away from this book, it is the powerful impact of planning. When you are armed with a comprehensive and actionable plan, you can make a huge difference in your retirement happiness and financial success. Make the right Social Security decisions, pick the right investment strategy, understand the risks you face, get insurance when it fits your plan, take the right distribution option from your qualified plan, create a tax-efficient withdrawal strategy, and don't be afraid to get professional advice. If you take these steps, you can improve your retirement security, create peace of mind, and live the kind of retirement you have always hoped for. Remember—rewire the way you think about retirement planning to have a happier and more financially secure future.

About the Author

J amie P. Hopkins, Esq., MBA, LLM, CLU, ChFC, CFP, RICP, is a professor of taxation at the American College of Financial Services and director of the American College New York Life Center for Retirement Income. As a professor, he has educated thousands of financial services professionals and continues to move the needle for retirement income planning. Professor Hopkins was instrumental in the creation and development of the Retirement Income Certified Professional (RICP) education program. As a retirement income planning expert, Professor Hopkins educates financial advisors on retirement planning best practices.

As the Larry R. Pike chair in insurance at the American College, Professor Hopkins focuses his educational content on thought leadership, development, consulting, and speaking, with respect to the areas of retirement income planning. He has also made it a life goal to get these best practices out to consumers. Professor Hopkins's work has appeared in numerous research publications, including *Forbes*, *WSJ*, *Barron's*, and the *Economist*.

Professor Hopkins is considered one of the leading retirement planning experts in the United States and was selected by *InvestmentNews* as one of the top forty financial services professionals under the age of forty. He was also recognized by the American Bar Association (ABA) as one of the top forty young attorneys in the country.

Professor Hopkins received his BA in political science at Davidson College and his JD from the Villanova School of Law, where he graduated with honors.

He later received an MBA from Villanova University Business School and an LLM from Temple University. Professor Hopkins also holds the Certified Financial Planner (CFP), Chartered Life Underwriter (CLU), Chartered Financial Consultant (ChFC), and Retirement Income Certified Professional (RICP) designations.

Made in the USA
Middletown, DE
30 May 2018